The Conjurer's Almanaq
by Roy Leban and Emily Dietrich

Published by Almanaq LLC
Redmond, Washington USA

www.almanaq.com

Limited Edition, November 2018
First Mass Market Edition, January 2019

This page is not part of any puzzle
Hints, assistance, and answer confirmation is available at www.almanaq.com/hints
Subscribe to our newsletter at www.almanaq.com/newsletter
Use hashtag #almanaq on social media

793.73 / GV1507

ISBN 978-0996256810

The Conjurer's Almanaq

by The Great Qdini

FOR ANYWHERE'D TJGTYTM SD

PRPSATFRP XSFO BERTF TZZERASTFSNY

FN TJJ NK NHE VSAVDFTEFRE QTAVRED

Introduction

Splendid! Your yearning for knowledge has led you to hold The Conjurer's Almanaq in your hands!

This volume is remarkable and unique (if I may be forgiven for that immodest assessment). In it, I transgress the custom of protecting the protocols and procedures of conjuring from the public. I have no fear of exposure, for what have I to lose? I know well that my prowess cannot be surpassed, so I can be generous with secrets. I am so bold as to hope that the contents herein will be of use to or inspire those who would embark upon the remarkable and rewarding journey of conjuring.

I first implore you to search your heart for your own motivations. If you seek to gain admiration, or the favor of amore, or, most importantly, riches, reconsider this undertaking! Conjuring creates calisthenics for the mind and delivers delight to the heart: these rewards suffice for true devotees of the conjuring arts!

I hope herein to provide guidance and mentoring to you, as my mentor did to me. Although we parted ways when I came to believe that public displays of the arts were less beneficial to the world than using them to serve a larger purpose, I will always be grateful to him and want to pass along my knowledge as he generously did with me. By creating this Almanaq, I hope to educate many where my mentor could educate only a few.

Each chapter of The Conjurer's Almanaq begins with general descriptions and histories of a key aspect of conjuring followed by detailed, practical, and specific methods you can use, with the intent of giving you the best possible results. These are not just generic instructions, but ones I have carefully honed over the years for maximum effectiveness, including the clues you need for success. Your own effectiveness depends upon your willingness to be meticulous in your procurement of supplies and in the manner of your preparations. As you learn the arts, you should take detailed notes — you never know when they might come in handy.

Although some conjurers eschew using outside resources in their studies, most conjurers use everything they could get their hands on. Historically, conjurers have made use of sundials, codexes, the *Naturalis Historia*, even what is now known as the Rosetta Stone. Today, conjurers are more likely to use modern technology such as slide rules, sextants, and the web of pages.

You may understandably feel a sense of urgency in learning the conjuring arts. But, there is no clock running, no time limit. Since different conjurers will find different arts easier and harder, you must choose your own path to mastering the arts, in whatever order works best for you.

Above all, you must maintain your inner calm and resist the urge to tear apart this volume as you go. Your absolute focus is required as you work your way toward metamagic, that most advanced art in which conjurers combine everything they've learned in order to accomplish inconceivable things.

I wish you a challenging and enlightening journey as you venture into the realm of conjuring!

The Great Qdini

If you're reading this, it's too late!
You're already trapped in this book.

The Great Qdini put a spell on The Conjurer's Almanac!

I was his first victim, but I was able to get out.

So there is hope for you!

My secret was that I had learned Qdini's true name years ago. That will be your key to defeating his spell. I have secretly modified this book to place a puzzle in every chapter. They're hidden, so you have to find them before you can solve them!

You don't have to write within the Almanac or tear out any pages to solve anything.

Once you've solved the 10 essential puzzles, combine them to learn Qdini's true name. With that, you will be able to uncover the counterspell. Speak the counterspell out loud 5 times quickly to break out of this book!

Best of luck to you!

Table of Contents

Symbology

Symbols have long been thought to be human-made, but this is not entirely correct — the truth is more complex. Early humans found models for symbols around them in nature, and they replicated and reproduced them in cave drawings, then on papyrus, on paper, and eventually on digital devices.

Worldly Symbols

Humanity evolved and so did symbols. Symbols that originally were crude became more defined. As a result, symbols and their relationships to each other effectively became a part of human life on earth, sending power in all of the compass directions.

Symbols found in the world vary greatly, from marks on trees to elegant crop circles. Those symbols which are more permanent are more powerful. Crop circles are the least permanent and therefore are the weakest. Customarily, only a few conjurers can absorb power from a crop circle before it is depleted, inert. As a result, it is hard to discern the difference between a real crop circle and a fake one. On the opposite end, those symbols forged in stone contain rare permanent power. Like unlimited batteries, stone symbols give every conjurer who uses them the full range of power when they signal them. Eight of these stone symbols are presented here.

Symbols, to be conjured, must be signaled at will, quickly and expeditiously, drawn on paper or other impermanent objects. The more power a symbol has, the more precise the copy must be, so accuracy is particularly important with powerful stone symbols. In prehistory, conjurers used stone rubbings; some can be found in historical archives. *Things have changed!* With today's technology, if one encounters a stone symbol in nature, a snapshot or selfie is recommended. Images get posted to Twitter or Facebook, for example, complete with hashtags which are opaque to laypeople.

Symbol objects shouldn't ever be moved away from their original GPS locations lest they lose power. Power absorbed from a symbol object that has been moved will be lost forever!

15

Light

FIRE, FLASH

The *Light* symbol is used to light up an object or an area. It can illuminate an entire small room, or, for instance, a cave. It has been used as a distraction or misdirection during stage shows with quite satisfactory results. The light resulting from this symbol is bright and hot.

STAR *w/STARS, ⚡ STARRY*

The famous conjurer Astral Constella, used the Light symbol to solve her fifth case as a consulting detective. Having found a kidnapped heiress, she used the Light symbol to guide the constabulary to her location. With that bright light in place, Senora Constella pursued the kidnappers in their fast and frantic flight and brought them to justice without endangering the heiress further!

FIRE + GLASS

Light and Lock can work together to create light that will follow a moving object, human, or animal, like a spotlight. This can prove useful in a stage show, which conjurers pretending to be magicians have sometimes used. Conversely, Light and Lock can keep people from being able to hide. They were used together famously in a chase at sea, enabling the captain of a vessel to keep eyes on the nefarious pirates who had been hired to steal magical cargo. The incident resolved with the cargo back in the rightful hold!

lock spotlight

NORTH STAR

rl + ws LIGHT

Always

TIME ?
MEMORY

The *Always* symbol is almost the power of forever. Many a conjurer has wished Always worked for true love or fairness, justice or success! Alas, only upon objects or functions will this work, not on wishes and dreams.

Nevertheless, the power of Always has its uses. It makes something happen constantly or repeatedly. It can also make something that was brought into existence through conjuring continue to exist indefinitely. Applying the symbol to an object also makes that object indestructible: it will always exist.

When the Abyss symbol is used on an object already under the power of Always, the object becomes again a mutable object, without any power of being everlasting and immutable. The same is true when an Always symbol is used on an object already under the power of Abyss, whether they have just been introduced to the symbol, or they are using it for the seventh time.

Echo

MIRROR

Echo produces a duplicate. The power of Echo can duplicate sounds, as natural echoes do, but it can also duplicate objects and visions.

Used properly, Echo can make it appear as if there are many copies of an object. The great conjurer Enchantra used this effectively in a triumphant encounter with thieves. She had raided the thieves' lair to retrieve cadmium they had stolen from her and was fleeing. Outnumbered, she hid in an alley and used Echo over and over again on a nearby cat, creating the illusion that the alley was filled with yowling cats. As eager as they were to retrieve the cadmium, by the time the eighth angry cat appeared, the thieves were more than happy to vacate the alley, leaving Enchantra free to go on her way.

When Abyss is added to Echo, the result is a "dark echo," a black cat when a white cat is copied, or, a bit surprisingly, a mirror where a pane of glass is copied. In the latter case, the addition of Abyss causes a side of the glass to become pitch black, resulting in a mirror effect.

Never

Never is the power of negation. Never prevents something from happening, or it can prevent something that has happened from happening again. Never has been misused and misunderstood as long as people have wanted to have control over their lives.

The power of the symbol Never can also be used to try to prevent illness, tragedies, death. But humans are poor soothsayers. We *imagine* we can predict the dangers that might befall those we love. Whatever Never is used to protect against, there are many, many, *many* other unpleasant and terrible things that can happen, perhaps even more unbearable given the knowledge of all that was prevented. There is no documented success of Never's power being used to make a human happy, though it has been used, for a time, to keep a human safe.

A second use of the power of the symbol of Never can be made by combining it with Lock. Using these symbols together makes it impossible to duplicate something. Conjurers have used them to protect a key to keep their treasures safe. Conjurers have also used this combination to keep a secret, such as how to create a talisman or alchemical substance.

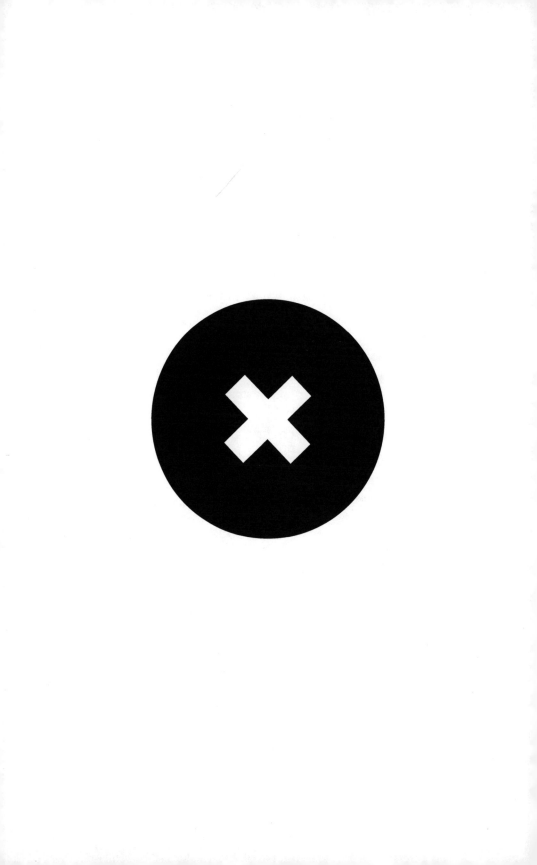

Abyss

SMOKE

The power of *Abyss* can block all forms of illumination, darken an area, and even project darkness. Abyss can work wonders in misdirecting an audience, a competitor, or a foe in combat. Abyss has been used dramatically by many a conjurer to hide or to abscond when necessary.

Enchantra, who uses symbols with great aplomb, tells the tale of a brilliant use of the power of the Abyss symbol. She was caught inside a room with no exit when trying to discover a spell from the conniving conjurer Egon Tistica, who had kept it hidden against the custom of the conjuring community. She had located the spell in a jar of cinnamon kept in Egon Tistica's root cellar. When he appeared at the top of the stairs, Enchantra used the power of Abyss to disappear in the shadows among potatoes and turnips. This allowed her to be almost invisible through the fourth time someone searched the root cellar. Later, she used Abyss again to slip away through the kitchen while the host dined with a table full of guests just a few feet away!

Perhaps paradoxically, when Echo is added to Abyss it can produce a sort of camouflage. Though temporary, a person cloaked with Echo added to Abyss can appear to be almost anything the conjurer desires.

SHADOW
MOON

MAGNET?

Lock

The power of the *Lock* symbol has been used in ingenious ways. On its face it is the power to make things sealed, inaccessible. It can also prevent powers from being used on an object. Many a conjurer has used Lock to seal a door or fuse a lock. Some people believe that the Egyptian Pyramids were sealed with Lock, which may be an indication that a Lock seal can last a long time, but not forever.

Lock is particularly interesting when combined with Mix, because the results are always hard to predict. Recently, an experiment was conducted to see if using Lock and Mix together could make a collection of items situated near to each other less accessible, in effect using Mix to spread the Lock effect and sacrificing the strength of the lock.

For this experiment, a book, a bottle of poison, and a mirror were used. The expected result was that the book would become indecipherable, that the bottle of poison would be sealed shut, and that the mirror would become dim and cloudy. Instead, the book was sealed shut, the poison became dim and cloudy, and the mirror became indecipherable. While this first test was quite interesting, clearly more testing is needed!

Mix

Mix is a wild card of the symbols. It is the power to scramble things, jumble them, turn them around. The possibilities of Mix are endless, because the results are different for every object, and the results are different when Mix is used with any other symbol.

Students of conjuring must develop their own lexicon of Mix effects through rigorous and meticulous experimentation. Results of the Mix symbol are not at this time consistent from conjurer to conjurer, causing speculation that perhaps each conjurer has their own Mix, so to speak. Some of the idiosyncratic results have been: causing an object to fall apart, fall down, or become inverted; jumbling the components of an object to create another object; mixing physical objects with each other, usually with disastrous results; muddling the writing of a document so as to make it unreadable; and scrambling eggs.

Mix pairs are understood somewhat better. For example, when Mix and Abyss are used together, the effect of Abyss is somewhat muted to about a sixth of its usual strength, which can be useful when it is desired to only partially conceal something, allowing a hint of its presence to remain.

Open

The power of *Open* can be a physical or metaphorical opening. It can be used as a universal key to open something. Or, it can be used to reveal something or force something to open. It can even be used to open eyes, in the sense of changing someone's mind or causing someone to have a realization.

The Open symbol functions in whatever manner is necessary to match the object to which it is applied. It will allow entry to any type of container or room, functioning in place of a key, a crowbar, or even an explosive. For locked containers such as boxes, chests, wardrobes, and warehouses, the symbol will have to be used on the lock and then again, if necessary, on the container itself. The heaviest object dispensed of by Open, of record, is a boulder weighing over a ton, which blocked a passageway under a coliseum. Possibly apocryphal accounts describe a sort of melting disintegration of the solid rock.

When the wild card symbol Mix is applied to Open, a certain amount of randomness takes effect. A door might unlock and relock sporadically, or the door might even vanish completely. Open and Mix might be applied to a pair of items, and a third, seemingly unrelated item, opens itself. This might seem like a completely useless effect, but there are times when a conjurer might wish to introduce an element of surprise into a situation, and the combination of Open and Mix can accomplish that.

Spells

For centuries, conjurers have been casting spells in Latin, but this has never been required, and there are indeed spells which use common English words.

Spell Casting

 To properly cast a spell, the conjurer must focus on not just the most common words, but also the letters that make the words, and, of course, the meaning of the entire spell.

In learning about spell casting beyond mere common words, one may discover little snippets of text which merit greater emphasis. If these snippets are combined, overlapping them from spell to spell, a special phrasing may be discovered. While not a spell in its own right, such a phrasing can nonetheless have great power.

Although it can be tempting to translate a spell from Latin to English, or vice versa, translating a spell from its original language renders it useless. *Do not be tempted!*

It is important to dismiss a misconception about spells. Those new to conjuring think that all spells must be spoken out loud in order for them to work. *This is not true!* Although you may encounter a spell which must have its most common words spoken to work, almost all spells may be written instead, or even just thought. A beginning conjurer should not even think of speaking a spell out loud. Many common English words have multiple ways they can be pronounced, and even a single errant mispronunciation can produce disaster.

While counterspells are beyond the purview of this chapter, in fact, beyond the grasp of any conjurer who has not yet reached metamagic, it would be negligent to not point out some essential differences. Unlike spells, most counterspells *must* be spoken out loud in order for them to work, and, for reasons lost to the mists of time, most counterspells must be spoken backwards.

Utor laenae

atrita neque

adfulsi iens

Perceptibility

This spell, known in English as *Perceptibility*, is almost as useful as an invisibility spell, and it is infinitely more valuable because, unlike an invisibility spell, it actually exists. Like any perceptibility spell, this spell affects people, not objects. It affects what other people will see or not see. When properly applied, the conjurer will be like the bear behind the juggler, and simply be ignored.

Every spell has a time limit and will eventually wear off, but a spell of perception or concealment, and this one in particular, is very sensitive. Be careful, lest the spell wear off suddenly, revealing the conjurer at an inopportune time.

While conjurers can apply this spell to themselves, it is common to apply it to a garment, such as a cloak (hence the myth of so-called invisibility cloaks). Wearing such a spell-cast garment gives the full benefit of the spell, while allowing the conjurer to turn it on and off instantly.

Visitare aquae

phantasme

milium et

Liquefied Hydrogen Hydroxyl

Liquefied Hydrogen Hydroxyl is most uncommon — conjuring with a little bit of alchemy thrown in. It allows the summoning of water by intoning its Latin name. Here is a challenge to conjurers to name any more effective method for summoning the beloved life-giving liquid than this one!

An ill-fated colleague, whose name was El Grande Cognomen, often tried to use Greek intonations, but an amazingly powerful whirlpool, conjured by his own mouth, sucked him under forever.

Another colleague, by the name of Mariposa Magica, prefers Japanese. Her spells are effective but unreliable, and she has twice been disappointed (and endangered) by the trickles conjured up when she needed a spate, a river, or even a cataract!

To name another conjurer with an odd predilection, the famed conjurer by the name of Dazzling Dani persists in casting Finnish-language spells, though she can't name even one word in Finnish. Respectable conjurers name her among the worst conjurers known since she effectively steals water from deep aquifers instead of producing her own, a practice widely considered by conjurers of quality to be unethical.

Therefore, adherence to Latin is preferable.

Freezing

Freezing has incredible raw power. Conscientious conjurers must ponder long the lengths to which they will go to achieve their goals before casting it. Results are difficult, if not impossible, to control without also casting an aqueous spell as a backup.

Conjurers measure freezing in both degrees and lengths, or fathoms, of ice. This fact should be a warning about significant dangers; lengths are used because freezing is about both temperature and volume. The first conjurer who cast Freezing was not very good at math, particularly geometry, hence one-dimensional lengths instead of three-dimensional volumes.

There once was a student who would go to any lengths in practicing his casting. He (who shall remain nameless here) cast Freezing in a remote area, in an ill-fated attempt to destroy an old building. He surrounded the building with a ring of ice, but it didn't stop there. The temperature dropped and the ice spread, capturing an adjacent stream. Before he could summon warmer water, the ice had reached 80 lengths, almost 500 feet in all directions, killing vegetation in a huge area.

Aside from volume, be advised that temperature drops can happen suddenly and unexpectedly. Absolute zero means certain death. Even if a conjurer goes to great lengths, these effects are irreversible.

Unimaginable Happiness

Unimaginable Happiness is a boon for those who suffer, despair, or even wallow. Here, cast-ees, rather than casters, indicate the quality and type of bliss summoned.

Therefore, conjurers may not use Unimaginable Happiness on one they do not know. This sad anecdote can indicate possible unforeseen consequences. A conjurer once cast Unimaginable Happiness, thinking they knew what kind of person they were dealing with, but the bliss that followed was not what past experience with the person would indicate. The individual was quite enamored of baby animals, and upon casting, all manner of baby beasts promptly appeared. His brusque manner and profession as a drill sergeant did not at all indicate that this would happen. His resulting emotion was utterly satisfactory (one might even say euphoric), but clean-up tasks were not, nor was the necessity for searching out exotic animal adoption venues. The built-in-warning words (Latin "hue" which means "forever") indicate this caveat.

Unlike others, this one works better if conjurers indicate to subjects that they will be casting it. Request, if possible, that cast-ees indicate specific and potential sources for happiness in their dreams and fantasies.

At heia

relido liqueo

theatrum

Disorder

Disorder has a delightful inner irony. Although its effect is an appearance of chaos, the method is anything but random! It disorients a subject by having their brain switch around the positions of objects in a given space. Note that objects will not actually switch positions, but will appear to do so *only to the subject.* It should be noted, then, that this effect works *only inside a very specific room or enclosed area.*

To cast Disorder, you must make some very specific decisions and designations beforehand. Choose object pairs in opposite positions across a specific space, for example, an ash tree and a boulder, an accordion and an easy chair, or perhaps an atlas and an urn in appropriate positions. While intoning the words, subtly gesture toward both positions. The subject will now believe that the objects have switched positions.

This has been useful for escapes, retrieval of stolen items, and fights involving weaponry. For example, Saladdin related that her use of it has given her opportunities to occupy positions of advantage in physical confrontations with opponents who possessed much greater physical strength than she.

An important word of warning, however. Since no objects have actually changed positions, a casting conjurer must not do something which inadvertently reveals reality.

Fervo afa
tot ah
subex narravi

Shifting Ground

Shifting Ground has many ingenious uses! Here are two wonderful examples, where its use may seem surprising. The conjurer Delania de Landress lived in Kalamazoo, Michigan, where an important triennial piano competition occurs. One desperate virtuoso wanted his win to be less a matter of skill than of will. He paid Delania to conjure his victory. In the competition's finals, Delania cast Shifting Ground to move the stage ever so slightly under the piano where her client's rivals were playing. Very subtle! For one brief moment, or maybe two, during each performance, pianists' fingers were not where they needed to be, just enough to skew, sour a few notes, and throw off rhythm.

Another particularly interesting use, ages ago, was where subtlety was not a factor at all. Famed conjurer Die Majestik used it in 1692 to devastate an entire town. His patron, a British plantation owner, was impeded in increasing his empire by a town that sat where he wanted more sugar cane fields. Die Majestick intoned Shifting Ground, causing an earthquake that resulted in the town's land temporarily becoming quicksand. Buildings and people vanished, sucked down where fertile soil was dissolved by the earth's motion.

Cm ens pol
si futura
haec verbi duco

Language

Language conjures in two different ways. It can make people hear something different from what was said, or make people say something different from what was intended. In other words, it can affect what goes in one's ears, or what comes out of one's mouth. The power of spoken words, good conjurers know, is derived from specific sounds produced by bigrams and with bigrams, not by mere groups of letters.

This should be obvious to anyone who has heard the Jack and the Beanstalk story. Even a child can discern power in bigrams like "fē," "fi," and "fo."

Conjurer Jarona Japheera argues that it is trigrams, not bigrams, that is the basis of spells' effect. False! Bigrams comprise the smallest true phonetic unit. As proof — definite proof — note the bigrams "zu" and "mu" which by themselves can suffice to conjure Animal Utterances (too advanced for this volume). Japheera claims "zu" and "mu" are not bigrams, but trigrams "zoo" and "moo." Any competent conjurer (or orthographer, for that matter) knows that superfluous letters must be eschewed whenever possible. Her contention that "oo" spellings are superior because they clarify pronunciation is *obviously* ridiculous. Who needs a trigram when bigrams suffice?

Astral Protection

Astral Protection calls upon the healing power of stars and comes with two essential caveats: a conjurer who casts it *must* not be related to any subject, and must not start too soon. Even some professional conjurers have been known to start casting before it is necessary to help an ailing loved one. This is a recipe for double failure. A premature start can inhibit that natural healing which humans' bodies do.

Or worse. There was one conjurer, who will remain nameless to protect the innocent, who, at the first sign of suffering in his dear wife, would start casting Astral Protection. Because she was not a blood relative, it would work acceptably well. He could sometimes catch himself in time, recognizing risks, especially of an early intervention. But his distress at seeing his beloved suffer caused him to start too early when she merely had a terrible bout of intestinal gas. She was indeed in pain, terrible pain, but it would have been temporary. As a result, his wife gave a start and lost consciousness, and the powerful healing of the stars rendered her digestive track pristine inside — too pristine. Because of this, she had to start taking pills for cultivation of necessary bacteria and suffered from chronic digestive ailments galore.

When will conjurers start to take the wisdom, freely and unselfishly offered here to heart? Do not use on relatives! Start the process correctly by calling in a detached, disinterested conjurer instead.

Cards

From 3-card monte on South Beach to poker in East Las Vegas, playing cards have fascinated and engaged humanity's urges for fun and risk. *But conjurers have found far more interesting uses for cards!*

Playing Cards

 Conjuring with cards works through *plays*, the act of presenting one or more cards together. While a play can use any number of cards, up to a full deck, plays always start with one or two cards.

After initial cards define the nature of a play, other cards are added to complete it. With quintillions of possible plays, even experienced conjurers can play only a tiny fraction in their lifetime. It is almost as if a logic puzzle must be solved to figure out the best plays!

Each of the starting cards is dealt separately, creating stacks to which cards are added following simple rules. Always add an odd number of cards to a stack started with a Heart. In a play with two black cards of the same suit, always add an even number of cards to each stack. In a play that combines two different suits of the same color, add no more than two cards to one of the stacks.

Many card games rank the suits in power order. This is also true in card conjuring, with an explicitly defined power relationship. Clubs are the most powerful, Diamonds are valued at −1 (meaning 1 point less than an equivalently numbered Club), Hearts are valued at −2, and the least valuable Spades are valued at −3. The first time an Ace is used while making a series of plays, it is valued low (1); the second time, it is valued high (14). These values must be taken into account only when making plays.

At the end of the play, each stack is evaluated — the value of the starting card plus the number of cards played. A stack will never end up with a value greater than exactly half the number of cards in a standard deck. While some conjurers like to lay out plays in interesting ways instead of simple stacks, and it can be enjoyable, it has no impact on the play itself.

A Lone Ace

To many, lone Aces are the purest plays, and the most powerful Ace, the Ace of Clubs, is the purest play of all. It's one of the rare plays in which no additional cards are played.

When a lone Ace is played, it makes a sound. The quality of sound is akin to ventriloquism because the sound never seems to be coming from the location of the ace, but from somewhere else, somewhere nearby. Sometimes the sound seems to be coming from the next room or outside the door. With careful play, the experienced conjurer can even make the sound seem to come from underground! The sound created by this play can be counted upon to do at least one thing: distract attention.

Different suits produce sounds of increasing intensity. Many a squeak has come from playing an Ace of Spades. Some conjurers have described the sound of the Ace of Hearts as a book dropping or a handclap. The Ace of Diamonds sound level can be compared to a firecracker or a gunshot. As with so many of the conjuring arts, this one asks for skill and superb assessment of what precisely is needed!

The Ace of Clubs goes further, however. When the Ace of Clubs is the Lone Ace, it demands investigation. The sound will boom or crash, compelling those who hear it to find out what made the sound. A few conjurers have reported a deafening, thunderous sound, suggesting a cataclysmic event on par with an earthquake or eruption. The Ace of Clubs, then, can be counted upon to clear the room!

A Black Pair

The black suits are the most powerful and the least powerful suits, which makes black pair plays easy to control.

Black pair plays are used to produce a breeze. Strategically directed, a breeze can create the illusion of the presence of someone behind a curtain. A breeze can turn pages, or make a light object disappear from a surface. A breeze could rouse someone from a nap or a reverie, make someone sneeze, muss hair, cause a chill, or even change a mood.

The combination of the Three of Clubs and the Five of Spades starts a spiraling puff of air, with an average of nine more cards in each stack required to complete the play. These cards must be added carefully to get exactly the desired outcome. The puff from this play crescendoes into a very brief gust of sufficient strength to snuff a candle out.

With different ranks, varying types of breezes result. The conjurer will need to experiment over time to learn the subtle differences. With this play, the space where the play will be made must be taken into account. The stiffest breeze comes from paired face cards. These breezes are swift and intense, but very brief. It is said that El Magnifico of Spain used this play to doff the hat of a thief, under which was hidden the hostess's prized topaz and diamond tiara! One important caution about these plays: it takes months of practice to manipulate the plays to result in the breeze coming from a specific direction. When precision is necessary, ample preparation will be required!

A Red Pair

The red suits are the middle power suits, and their closeness in power makes red pair plays more accurate though harder to control than black pair plays. These plays conjure an odor.

Plays starting with the Three of Hearts and the Ace of Diamonds need an average of nine and a half additional cards for each stack to complete the play. This play causes an odor that was described by Ophelia the Oracle as the odor of ten thousand memories. Occupants of the same room, under the influence of this play, will claim to perceive a smell of sea, of warm brick, of taffy, of pine, of perfume. Those whiffs lead people to leave their seats, the room, and even the area to search for the source of the smell that brings to mind an ineluctable moment in their past. In short, a subtle but useful chaos comes about, making everyone around preoccupied and pensive.

With low red pairs, an odor is produced that smells suspicious. It is an odor that Henry David Thoreau, a prodigious conjurer indeed, described as that of goodness turned bad. This odor can be used to transform the mood of a room, and has even been used to spark arguments and, reportedly, fisticuffs! Middle red pairs are played to conjure an odor of sulfur, or, more generally, to conjure a stench. A stench can derail almost any activity, from a card game, to a dinner party, to a show, or even an elaborate crime! One thief was discovered when, from his hiding place, he could not help but exclaim, "What is that smell?" The highest red pairs conjure the aroma of the subjects' favorite food, anything from cookies to steak to kimchi!

A Pair of Spades

Although Spades are the least powerful cards, a pair of them causes people to fall asleep. This particular Spades play, with the relatively distant Two and Eight takes an average of an additional seventeen cards in each stack to complete it.

When completed, this play can cause people nearby to fall asleep for several minutes. Just a quick nap, as it were. Consider the furniture! One conjurer used this play and caused his subject to break his nose when his head hit an oak armrest! The sleep is deep and impossible to interrupt until the time has elapsed. Upon waking, the subject will not remember having fallen asleep and will have neither seen nor heard anything that happened during that interval.

The lower the cards, the fewer the people can be affected by this play, and the shorter the length of their sleep, from seconds to perhaps an hour or more. The quality of the sleep is similar to a light nap. It has been used to divest a subject of an object in their possession, for example, and, in such a case, a light touch and a swift motion will be necessary, since the longest nap of this type is mere seconds! The royal Spades can affect a small roomful of people with a deeper slumber, complete with dreams, for about an hour. Still, the people must be in close proximity, and must be situated — before the play is made — so that they can slide safely into a sleeping position. Luckily, with this play, the subjects' minds immediately lose consciousness, but the muscles take longer to relax. Conjurers have a few minutes to arrange limbs and cradle heads before the body collapses.

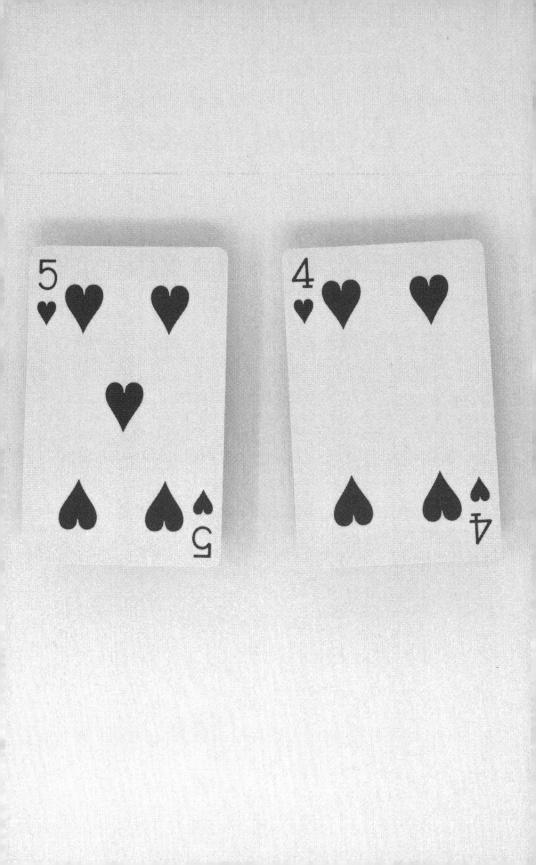

A Pair of Hearts

A pair of Hearts, fittingly, makes people amorous. Plays starting with adjacent Hearts, like the ones shown here, require, on average, the addition of sixteen cards to each stack.

This Five of Hearts and the Four of Hearts play creates a very special love mood in the room. With these two cards, a platonic love affecting every living entity in the room permeates the space. The effect does not last forever; enemies will feel kindly disposed to each other for about an hour. Snarling dogs have behaved like loyal companions greeting a returned master. Family holiday gatherings, known to resemble mine fields, become warm, fuzzy, and hug-filled, a useful effect in politically charged times.

With lower cards, the effect is the same but does not last half as long. Moving to the royal cards, we find romantic love begins to be part of the effect. As the presence of romantic love increases, predictability decreases. It has not been possible as of yet to ascertain how long the effect will last, nor if the effect will wear off completely. Some marriages are alive and well to this day due to the feeling generated by a Hearts play from many, many years ago. Also, it is impossible to designate which creatures, human and animal, will fall in love when these cards are played!

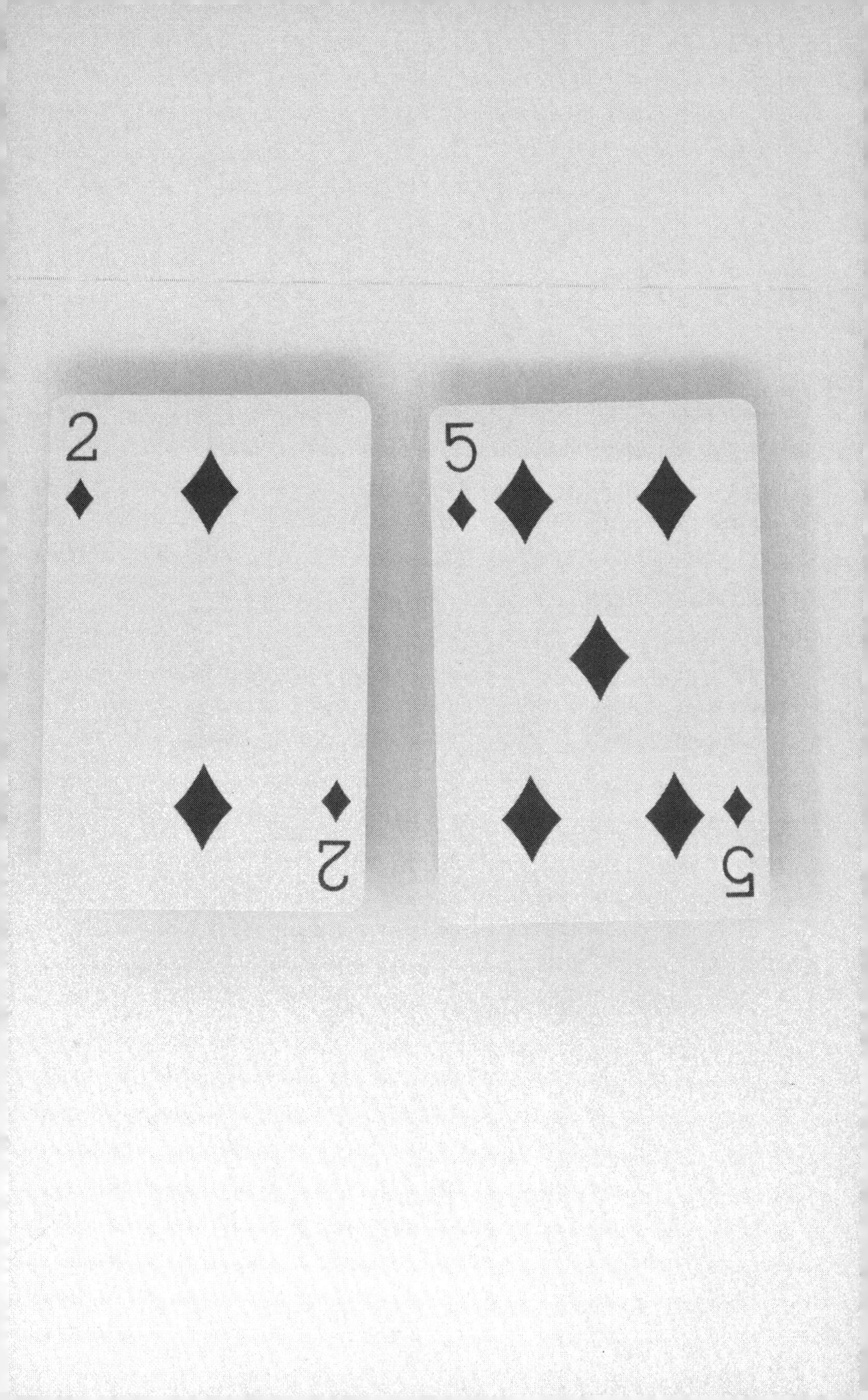
2
5

A Pair of Diamonds

A pair of Diamonds makes something fall over. With this Two/Five Diamonds combo, an average of fourteen and a half cards must be added to each stack in the play to complete it.

The strength of this play is ideal for creating a significant distraction without causing any meaningful damage. Conjurers have used this play to make a book fall from a shelf, a piano lid to slam shut, a vase of flowers to spill. Because the objects moved are not particularly heavy or large, those present do not suspect that conjuring has been employed, which can be an advantage in itself!

As the cards go higher, the objects caused to fall can be much bigger and much heavier. This play has been used to topple a smallish statue in a park, complete with the flight of frightened pigeons! Jay Hawke used this play to make a strongbox fall from its perch, through the floor to the floor below, where it burst open, revealing its secret contents.

It is little known outside conjuring circles that the implosion of Seattle's Kingdome was accomplished with a number of strategic Diamond plays rather than explosives. It was cheaper and safer, though the plays did not succeed in similarly imploding the debt still owed for constructing the stadium in the first place.

Although falling objects always present a risk of injury, with proper precautions, Diamond plays, whether targeted at books or stadiums, can be extremely safe.

A Pair of Clubs

A pair of powerful Clubs starts a machine, either mechanical or electrical. The Clubs pair shown here takes an average of nine more cards for each stack to be effective.

Clubs plays with middle cards start medium-sized machines. For example, remote activation of outboard motors has been reported, bringing watercrafts to aid elaborate circumventions. In another instance, a bonging grandfather clock has provided a convenient distraction. The element of surprise is effective, of course, but this play can also be part of a larger plan, for which some steps need to be initiated without the conjurer's presence.

Playing lower cards can start only very small machines such as a music box, a razor, a hair dryer, an alarm clock (or just the alarm). Machines such as these can give rise to a sense that a place is haunted by ghosts or inhabited by poltergeists. Royal cards aim the highest, activating machines as large as an automobile or bus, a carousel, a pipe organ, or perhaps a mainframe computer. Please advise the conjuring community with results from attempts to activate other large machines. No information is available on success or failure with locomotives, aeroplanes, or cement mixers.

A Mixed Pair

Mixed pairs, with one red suit card and one black suit card, are particularly powerful, providing a way to break something apart. There is some irony that the two least powerful suits, Hearts and Spades, can combine to create the most powerful plays, but only when an average of ten cards are added to each stack in the play.

Even the pair of the Two of Hearts and the Seven of Spades, one of the least powerful within this group, is quite powerful. This illustrates the strength of this play, and, one hopes, also brings attention to the necessity for caution when using it! This play can break apart most substances used in construction, effectively enabling the conjurer to destroy a house or small building. The Twos can break apart brick, wood, and stucco. Many walls have been felled with this play.

In the middle range, cards can break apart concrete and cement. A dramatic moment came when a conjurer used this play to breach a dam! Still higher cards can break apart a boulder. This ability renders even a medieval fortress vulnerable! The assiduous conjurer Kal Amazo used this play to construct a tunnel through the rocks near Lake Superior.

It has been reported that a mixed pair of royal cards, played properly, can even split a mountain. Supposedly, Yosemite's Half Dome is the result of such a play, but, as with many reports of early conjuring feats, it is unknown if this story is true or apocryphal.

Potions

Potions provide an entrée to conjuring for those less committed to the rigors of pursuing mastery. Potions forgive minor errors (mostly), and potions reward attempts with grand effects and results.

The Purpose of Potions

 The potions included in an able conjurer's repertoire differ from those of naturopathic practitioners or of chemists. While conjuring purposes include healing (and healing is a noble aim), neither conjuring nor potions exist for healing alone.

Similarly, while conjuring is not a capitalistic endeavor, many a conjurer has found it useful to use it to make money. Rare and unusual ingredients are expensive, which means that, of all the conjuring arts, potions is the one that is the most capital intensive.

Conjuring is its own purpose. Therefore the purpose of potions described here is as means to conjure. Why do this? One hopes the motives are pure, and perhaps only time will tell.

At any rate, if the tasks thus far in this volume have been found too daunting to attempt, this chapter may be the way to burgeoning confidence. Most abodes can accommodate the small space needed to carry out most of the recipes listed here. Potions are also the area of endeavor in which novices can be encouraged to concoct their own recipes. When appropriate, share the results. Many conjurers prefer to keep potions private. That is their right! But how much richer and robust the art and practice of conjuring becomes when discoveries are shared freely!

Finally, of the potions meant to be drunk, *only one* potion may be drunk at a time! Allow at least one day before drinking a different potion!

Right Brain Cocktail

This potion has a negative effect: left brain lethargy. The right brain will be performing magnificent creative stunts, which is the reason to imbibe the concoction created from the ingredients below. However, a corresponding diminishment of physical energy over the whole body also occurs, as well as a decrease in analytical abilities. Ideas will flood the brain! Discriminating between absurd and practicable ideas will be very difficult while under the influence of this potion.

Ingredients:

½ cup	Fish oil *(cold water fish preferable)*
1 tbsp	ground graphite
1 tsp	ground peach pit
1 tsp	extract of Icelandic poppy seeds
1	bird of paradise feather
1	bird of paradise petal
2 tbsp	Lemon juice
⅛ tsp	crystalized coconut husk

Mix dry ingredients first, then add fish oil and lemon juice, stirring briskly, then sprinkle in coconut husk. Drink before the graphite and peach pit grounds settle.

Forged Ink Mix

Whatever is written with this Forged Ink Mix potion will appear to the beholders to be legitimate. Whole forged documents as well as individual signatures will fool all concerned parties. It works on canvas as well as on all types of paper, authentic vellum excepted. By all means, share the results if attempted on any other materials! Note that this ink is not waterproof.

Ingredients:

7 tbsp	Liquefied soot
1 tbsp	crystalized henna
⅛ tsp	Extract of Dragon fruit
3 tsp	unsweetened durian juice
6 tsp	western Atlantic squid ink
2 tbsp	Nile river water

Mix squid ink and water, then add other ingredients, stirring well. Some potionmasters like to add a bit of perfume to mask the foul smell of durian juice. Use any perfume sparingly lest it ruin the ink.

Fade to Black Extract

This potion makes things invisible. It can make any thing invisible, but it cannot make a living being invisible. This potion makes a thick liquid, which must be rubbed all over the object to render it invisible. Take care to cover the whole object! There have been unfortunate attempts resulting in disastrous discoveries when a conjurer neglected to ascertain that every bit of the object was covered with the potion!

Collection of these ingredients takes advance planning. Experienced conjurers collect the ingredients in season every year.

Ingredients:

¼ tsp	Dried Hummingbird wings
½ tsp	powdered Alpine mayfly wings
¼ cup	Liquefied dandelion seeds
1 tsp	French plum blossoms *(chopped)*
1 cup	Fresh snow *(loosely packed)*

Mix all the ingredients into the snow, stirring constantly until the snow turns into water. Take care that all the ingredients are fully mixed in before any of the snow becomes water, lest the mixture become volatile.

Pure Color Changing Drops

The Pure Color Changing Drops potion will change the color of any object, organic or inorganic, animal, vegetable, or mineral. The color-changing process moves more quickly when applied to organic objects. For example, a head of hair could go from brown to magenta in ten minutes. Minerals and metals take more time. For example, a five-pound stone would take approximately two hours to change from gray to crimson.

The ingredients all come from plants and animals known for their camouflaging abilities, including milk of magnesia, which changes color when it comes into contact with acids. The recipe does not state a specific butterfly to be used — use any variety that is color changing, such as a Green-banded Swallowtail or a Blue Morpho.

Ingredients:

1 cup	Ink from a Live octopus
1 cup	milk of magnesia
¼ tsp	dried Leopard skin
1	Emerald spalding feather
1	mantis shrimp eye
¼	Dried chameleon claw
1 pair	Butterfly wings

Mix dry ingredients; then combine with milk of magnesia and octopus ink.

Ocean Pearl Tincture

The Ocean Pearl Tincture makes a nondescript object appear valuable and desirable. If it is dull, this potion makes it shine. If it is bumpy, it becomes smooth and sleek. The effect can serve as a distraction or as a temptation. The object can be used to lure someone into a trap or to bribe someone. Conjurers have used this potion when caught without money to make ordinary garments appear luxurious, then used them for trade.

Ingredients:

½ cup	Olive oil
½ cup	avocado oil
½ tsp	Tea tree oil
1 cup	rainwater
¹⁄₁₆ tsp	Titanium dust
1 tbsp	Lavender leaves
1 tbsp	rainbow Eucalyptus bark
1	abalone shell *(powdered)*

Mix oils and water until well blended, and then sift in other ingredients, adding abalone shell last.

Elixir of Shield Strength

More of a paste than a potion, this unique elixir channels the properties of plants and animals that have effective methods of shielding themselves. The resulting elixir can be used on both objects and humans. It provides good resistance to blades, swords, and bullets, as well as some protection from fire and other less tangible weapons. The more used, the stronger the shield will be.

Ingredients:

1	Shield bug
3	Armadillo scales
¼ tsp	Rattlesnake venom
5	Echidna spines, freshly plucked
1 tbsp	crushed Dragon scales
1 tsp	pangolin blood
3 tbsp	Oak tree sap
3 tbsp	dandelion honey

Chop scales and spines, then mix well with rest of ingredients to make a paste. Use as-is if applying it to an object, such as a metal shield; add warm water to thin it out if it will be drunk.

Second Second Soda

For a limited time after it is drunk, Second Second Soda allows one to see the second second in the future simply by closing the eyes. By closing only one eye, both the present moment and two seconds in the future can be seen simultaneously. It will take some getting used to, but even a mere two seconds of precognition can be a very powerful ability, and Second Second Soda is much easier to use than more sophisticated methods. When the vision fades, simply take another sip. Be careful not to drink too much or both the present and the future will become blurry.

Ingredients:

4	Tamarind seeds *(finely chopped)*
2 tbsp	Sassafras root *(finely chopped)*
¼ tbsp	ginger *(finely chopped)*
3 tbsp	dried Apple chips *(finely chopped)*
3 cups	fresh Northern spring water
3 lbs	Dry ice (carbon Dioxide)

Blend everything but the carbon dioxide and allow to sit for 1 hour hidden under a large rock. Strain the mixture, add the carbon dioxide, stirring well; then pour into a glass bottle or canister and seal it. Wait at least 24 hours before consuming.

Mash of Qi

This potion is unusual in two ways. It is one of the very few potions that are alcoholic, and it works on emotions. The Mash of Qi produces a feeling of tenderness both for and from the living being who has drunk it. It is not of use with inanimate objects. The quality of the tenderness ranges from gentle to adoring. It has many times moved from tenderness to affection to true love. But it is not a love potion. It is better! As a mash, it is also very thick, much thicker than most potions. It is to be applied behind the ears.

Ingredients:

> 2 tbsp powdered Astralagus leaves
> 1 tbsp crumbled Sumatran Hibiscus leaves
> 2 tbsp crushed goji berries
> 1 tsp   crystal malt
> 2 tbsp rolled oats
> 1 tsp   Elderberry Syrup
> ½ cup plum wine

First mix the leaves together. Then, in a separate vessel, mix berries, malt and oats. In a third vessel, mix the syrup and wine. In a fourth, larger vessel, combine the three mixtures and mix them together into a mash by hand.

Telepathy

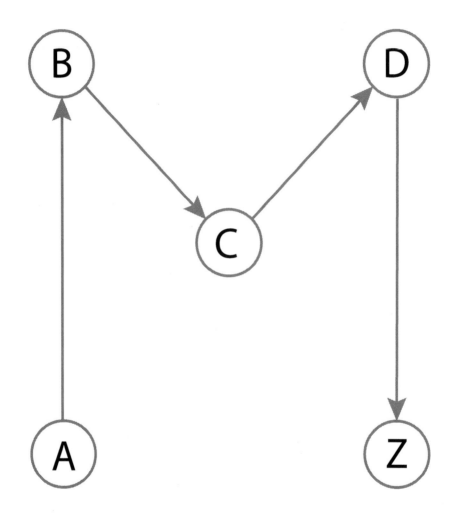

To the layperson, telepathy is merely a parlor trick of mind reading. To a skilled conjurer, however, telepathy is a whole host of skills, which serve to open up the mind wide, allowing one to see through the brain.

Opening Words

 In ancient times, it was thought that the brain was like a gate — words were outside the gate and thoughts were inside it. Within the gate, the most valuable items were hidden within walls.

With the advent of the industrial age, such preconceived notions were held up to the light of day. Views changed, and people began to understand that the brain was like a mathematical machine. Today, a better metaphor is a modern computer, a roomful of digital hardware packed into a mass of cells. This understanding is critical to telepathy, because only through mathematics and algorithms can a conjurer see their objectives clearly.

In tangible form, telepathy combines formulas and flowcharts. Some beginning conjurers believe the formula is more important while others believe the algorithm represented by the flowchart is more important. The truth is that they are of equal importance — combining them with the appropriate perspective is the key to success in telepathy.

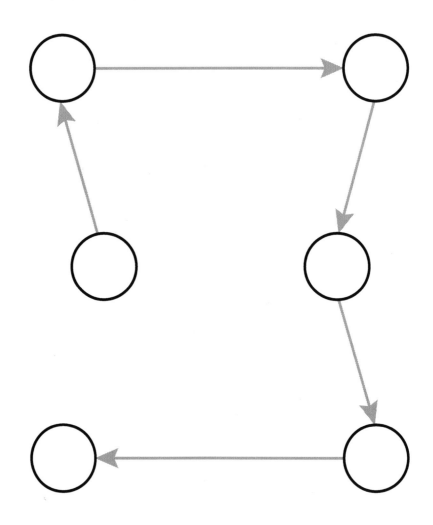

Thoughts

$$9 > e + \pi + \mathcal{N}$$

Hold up that thought! Nothing is more fundamental to math in the Western world than the integers, and every integer has its own relationship to the brain, as represented by its compositional formula. Anybody skilled in the art of mathematics will intuitively understand that the relationship between the integers and the transcendental constants of the universe is the key to reading somebody's thoughts.

This formula is able to unlock the reading of thoughts through its incorporation of the fundamental transcendental constants of the universe, e and π.

With the formula in mind, the process is straightforward.

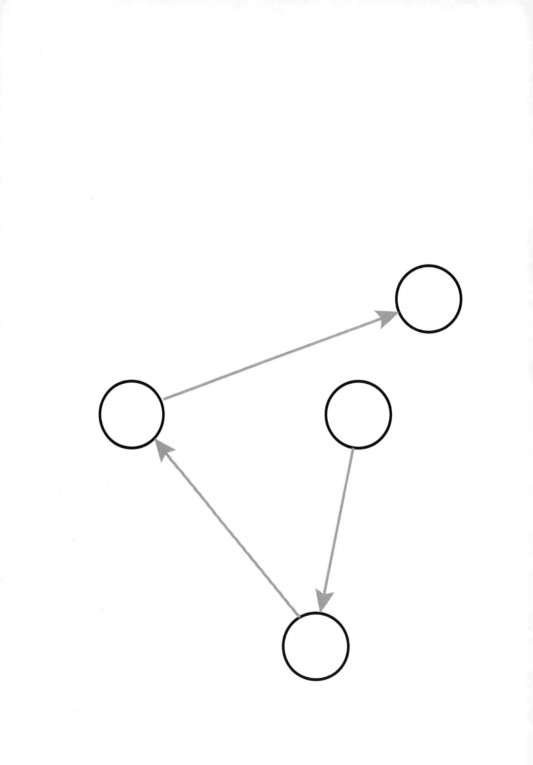

Words

$$\mathbb{R} + Я = \infty^3$$

Flowcharts can make the art of telepathy seem simplistic, but it is anything but! Words without thoughts can be the bane of creativity, while the relative independence of words and thoughts can be very useful in understanding and controlling people.

In conjunction with the previous formula, this formula allows the insertion of words into somebody else's mind. If the words are carefully chosen, the subject's mind will transparently create thoughts around those words and truly believe the thoughts are their own.

Be careful not to try to transfer more than nine words at a time as it can cause headaches, which will interfere with the formation of the desired thoughts.

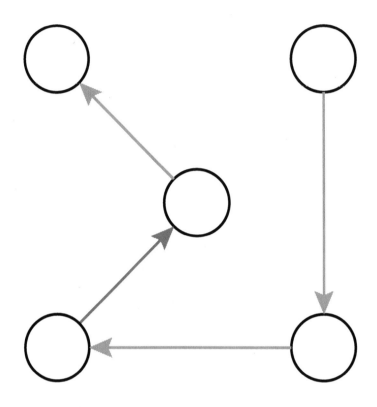

Opinions

$$\int r_0 = O_r - \int \pi r_0$$

Up in our brains, opinions often masquerade as thoughts, but they are usually emotions wrapped in false logic. Many humans confuse their opinions with their beliefs, and act according to their opinions instead of according to their beliefs. Another curious aspect of opinions is their effect on relationships. They can ruin them! Also, humans fight over their opinions often and vehemently. It seems irrelevant to humanity that there is no accounting for opinions.

To influence opinions through telepathy, the conjurer must gather opinions from the perspective of each of the seven traditional emotions. Opinions, which matter so little, can't hold up to the power of telepathy, risking pain or injury to the subject's mind unless the force is dispersed among a group of them. Changes made to opinions through telepathy can be seen through, which means they will not last long. Plan ahead!

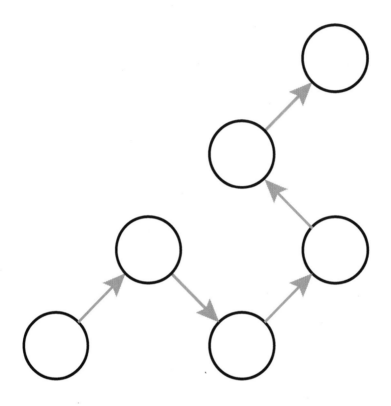

Dreams

$$c^2 = T^2 + \star\, t^2$$

To aspiring conjurers, dreams might seem like the perfect time for telepathy. To a large extent, this is true, but using telepathy to influence dreams can be done only when the intention of doing so results in something beneficial to the subject. It also must be done repeatedly — at least eight days in a week is generally considered to be an appropriate minimum.

In the early days of conjuring, it was discovered by the earliest known conjurer, Yourkis the Wise, that using telepathy to influence dreams for a harmful result yielded a permanent effect: subjects would from then on be visited by nightmares every time they were asleep, even the briefest catnap! Nightmares are bad enough, but the worse consequence was that subjects desperately avoided sleep, so scared were they of the nightmares that they had looked through. *Do not use telepathy to change dreams to the detriment of the subject!*

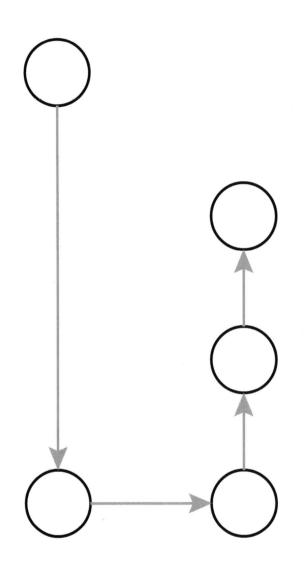

Ideas

$$e < 3 < \tau > 0$$

Light thoughts are ideas! This very simple statement starts a deep understanding of the difference between a thought and an idea. On a more technical level, ideas have considerably less energy than thoughts, less of an electrical charge. This makes them less fully formed and allows them to move quickly from place to place in the mind, which is the reason for the creativity of ideas.

The movement of ideas requires conjurers to be very careful. They must shine a light carefully, as it were, when using telepathy to create ideas. A possibly apocryphal story about a conjurer warns about this. A conjurer used telepathy to produce ideas in the mind of an oppressive feudal lord who was not accustomed to having ideas. He did this for eight days in a row. During this time, the ideas moved throughout the lord's mind, eventually reaching almost every region. The result was that the feudal lord became unable to think of anything but the ideas, and completely lost his ability to control his domain. Whether this was a good or a bad outcome is left as a thought exercise for the reader.

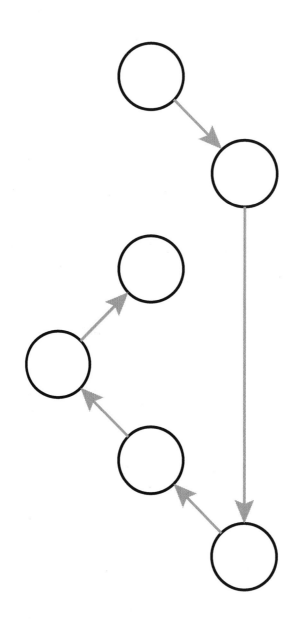

Meanings

$$\forall f_\varnothing \quad \exists \mathcal{S}_\varnothing \quad \Vdash \quad \Pi_1$$

To affect the perception of meaning, the conjurer needs to use telepathy on at most six subjects simultaneously, making this task somewhat more advanced. Meaning is created in a relationship between a perceiver and the perceived. For purposes of telepathy, the perceiver in the pair must be living, usually a human or an animal, or an entire audience taken as a whole. The perceived entity need not be living. The perceived entity can be an object, a building, a mountain, a human, or an animal, among other possibilities.

Using telepathy to create an interpretation of meaning has been used by conjurers around the globe to produce the perception that an object is conveying meaning to them, giving them an understanding of the object, animal, or person as being able to communicate without words. This is usually transparently seen by the perceiving subject as "magic."

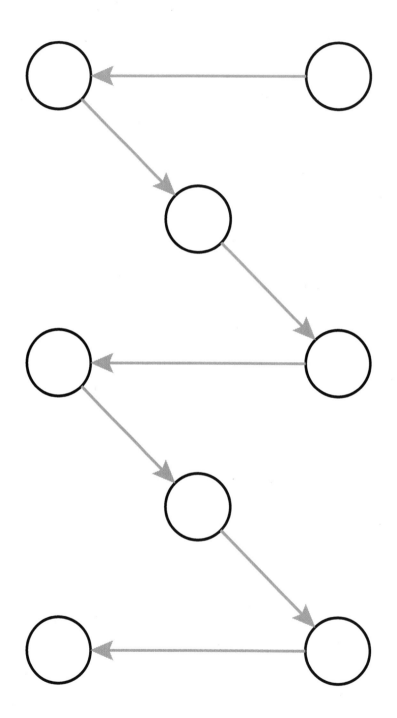

Feelings

$$\sum_{i=0}^{\infty} T^i \rightarrow 7$$

"Discover your feelings" has been a repeated mantra since people understood they had feelings. It combines the first pair of the six core mantras of discovery, feelings, respect, love, clarity, and vision.

The mantra resonates because feelings involve not just the mind, but the soul. Despite this added complexity, it may be a bit surprising to learn that producing feelings in a subject is not at all difficult. The connection between the mind and the soul is so close that it is almost easier to access mind and soul simultaneously than to access the mind alone. In fact, the conjurer must take care *not* to engage the soul when attempting telepathy to elicit the other effects listed in this chapter.

As is the case with many feelings, those brought about through telepathy are not long lasting, which is probably for the best for all concerned.

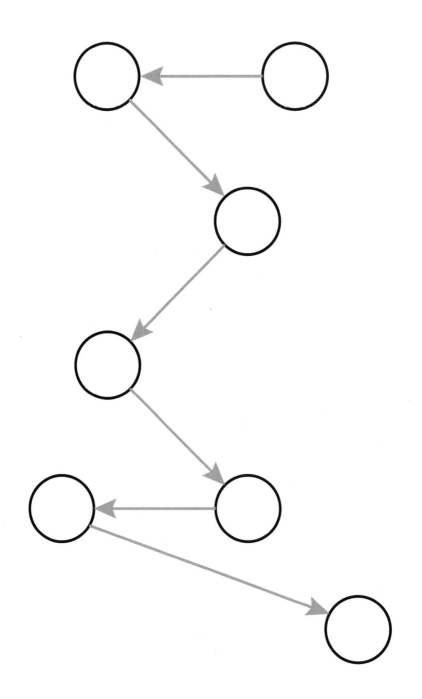

Beliefs

$$e^{i\pi} \lesssim 8$$

Letters like e and π represent transcendental constants, those numbers which are not algebraic and cannot be calculated with a finite algebraic formula. Transcendental numbers are so called because they transcend simple algebra to a realm of numbers beyond calculability. Contrary to popular belief, transcendental numbers are not rare, though mathematicians have deemed only four important enough to have single-letter names, the others being γ and Φ.

Like the numbers themselves, formulas that use transcendental numbers have the power to go beyond more normal formulas. This formula, using e and π combined with the inscrutable i, has the power to instill permanent core beliefs in a subject. It has long been rumored that this formula was used on magicians to prevent them from seeing through the difference between magic and conjuring!

Alchemy

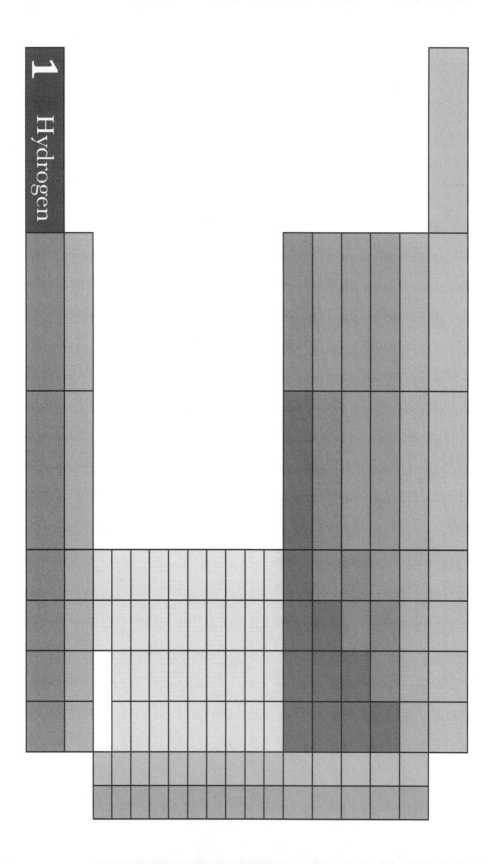

1 Hydrogen

Turning lead into gold was the original goal of alchemic exploration. That ancient pursuit has been greatly broadened by discoveries of new elements through the centuries. The true versatility of alchemy has been unlocked by combining multiple elements in a process known as melding, which allows the conjuring of far more than simple compounds.

Multi-element Alchemy

 Performing alchemy with multiple elements is very dangerous, and some mixtures may be volatile. It is therefore essential that elements be melded in the correct order as any other order may not be stable. *It is up to each conjurer to determine the correct order.*

The productions discussed in this chapter are the building blocks of alchemical conjuring. Conjurers who have mastered these building blocks can make almost anything. However, even with great skill, melding primary elements must be undertaken only as a final step, after all other melding is completed, to ensure that all compounds have a proper vessel. Again, determining the correct order is essential to avoiding a catastrophe.

Most of the elements used in alchemical preparations will have come into being on the earth through celestial events. These will be available to the reader through the usual channels of conjurers' commerce and trade. This volume does not provide methodology for the procurement of those elements not yet discovered at time of publication.

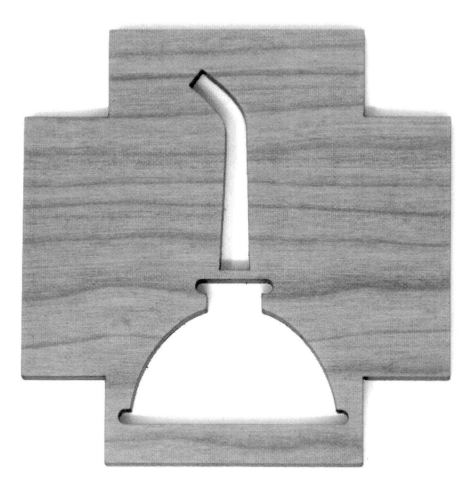

Oil

While oil is plentiful in the world, perfectly refined oil is another story. Most oil is impure, minus one or worse, treated with additives for different purposes, few of which are useful for conjuring purposes. When pure oil is needed, the best way to get it is to create it alchemically.

To ensure the oil is not too heavy, helium is essential. It is also colorless, odorless, and tasteless, which is helpful if the oil is to be used for conjuring food. However, using helium necessitates the development of techniques for working with undetectable substances.

Acquire iodine in its lustrous, purple-black solid form. Pay attention to the timing here, because iodine will need an hour of carefully monitored heating to bring it into proper form. Most importantly, the iodine must be heated to melting, but must never come to a boil!

Don protective breathing gear before introducing the asphyxiant nitrogen into the mix. The addition of potassium must be executed swiftly and skillfully: potassium reacts immediately with air.

Protective gear alone will not be sufficient for the technetium. Readers are responsible for researching and employing prudent practices in manipulating radioactive elements! Using sufficient wrist protection is an oft-overlooked practice!

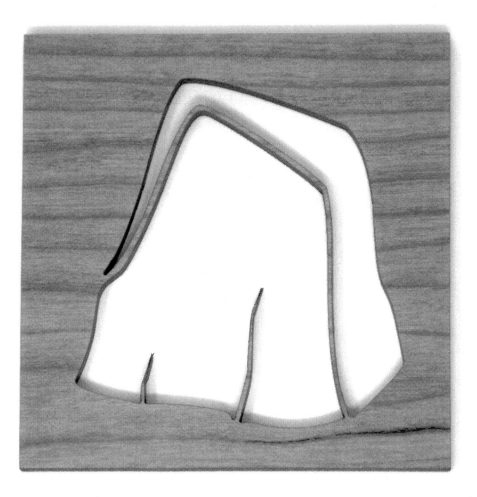

Stone

Alchemical stones have drawn attention since the discovery of the first two blue Sky Stones of Sierra Leone. Some cad of a conjurer irresponsibly created and abandoned a cache of attention-grabbing stones that attracted a great deal of research into their origins. Of course, stones can be created in different colors and sheens! That's child's play! But the ethical conjurer does not wish to advertise the supernatural origins of their creation! This combination produces a light gray stone. In this way, the stone's origins can be concealed if desired.

It is imperative to use beryllium from bertrandite, not from emeralds, red beryl, or aquamarine. That type will result in a hue far too strong, making the resulting stone appear to be magical or otherworldly. Use only potassium stored in paraffin oil for making stone to give the stones a silvery sheen. Lithium is used here for its heat resistance. Sulfur should be the meteoric type.

Oxygen, while essential to stone alchemy, must be used carefully. Whoever conjured the Sky Stones of Sierra Leone played fast and loose with oxygen in their process. They should have known the overuse of oxygen would create the remarkable color and texture. Most accomplished conjurers know better than to draw unnecessary attention to conjuring activities!

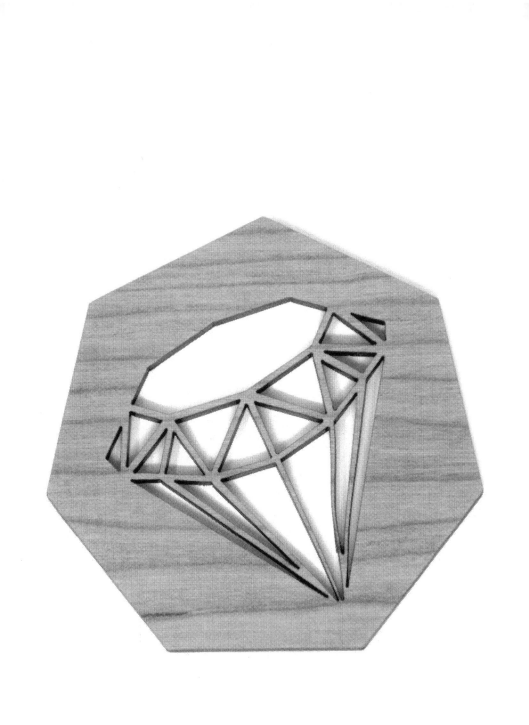

Diamond

The serious conjurer will not be creating diamonds through alchemy in order to promote romance, but in order to produce superlative mechanical inventions. Diamonds created this way have the lowest possible friction ratio and the highest possible electrical resistivity. The irreverent conjurer Jacko El Muerto attempted to woo the object of his affections with diamonds created with this method, but, like these diamonds, his would-be lover became more slippery and more elusive to his advances!

Nature makes a diamond from carbon alone, but it takes billions of years. Flawless alchemical diamonds can be made in a matter of hours, but require additional elements. Carbon from the upper layers of the troposphere is the most desirable for the conjurer's purposes. If that is not available, carbon from the stratosphere is the next best choice. If neither can be obtained, carbon extracted from an asteroid will suffice. It is best to extract potassium for alchemical diamond creation by burning wood or tree leaves in a grate. Place a pot in the ashes. Add water, heat, and evaporate the solution.

Cerium and lanthanum may come from the usual sources, but use a stainless steel knife with the cerium and protect fingers from the lanthanum. Leave out the Cerium and the result won't even reach a two on the Mohs scale!

A secret ingredient: Neon, born of the stars, enhances the luster of diamonds made by this method. Although these gems are made to be useful, what could be the harm in making them beautiful as well?

Earth

This earth is customized to encourage abundance and flourishing of crops and ores. It can also serve to dampen flights of fancy or provide the finest foundational support to architectural projects.

Astatine is the secret ingredient, this rarest of the elements in the earth's crust. Scientists have been unable to study astatine because of its brief half-life, but its enriching effect on earth's fecundity is known to practitioners of alchemy.

Students of conjuring are advised to begin cultivating a network of alchemists who can join forces to manufacture astatine as soon as they can. It will likely take years. The team will need to boast talents as varied as those needed to pull off a sophisticated bank robbery.

Nitrogen's properties as a fertilizer make it an obvious addition to a mixture to create earth. With its extremely high melting point, rhenium brings protection from fire and withering rays of the sun.

Compared to astatine, uranium exists in abundant levels throughout the world, though usually not in mineable quantities, and one must take great caution because its radiation can be deadly. Fortunately, this mixture only needs a tiny bit of uranium to call forth the power of nature in creating earth.

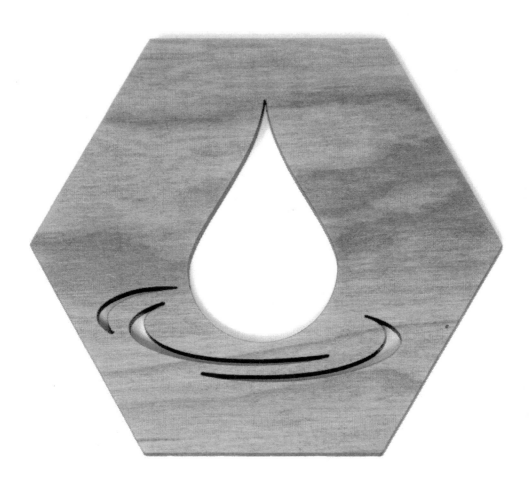

Water

Water has a calm, understated power. It can reflect or conceal, transform or stabilize, float something or drown it. With alchemically created water, all those powers are available. But one thing is certain: water created with alchemy is not for drinking.

Secret ingredient: nitrogen. Nitrogen has sometimes been called antiwater for its ability to choke breath. In some cases, adding a substance with the opposite characteristics adds power to an alchemical creation.

The element gallium is ideal for this mixture because it becomes a liquid at room temperature. Mere contact with the human body melts it. More than its liquidity, however, gallium's mirroring effect produces water of the kind that enhances perfection in reflected images and a clearer view to the beyond.

Germanium will not dissolve in water. It holds and displays light coming through it, so it remains in tiny precipitate in this alchemical product, an unusual effect. Sulfur, which is essential to all life, is essential to this alchemical water because this water reveals life, future lives, past lives.

Fire

From fire, a conjurer asks so much. To fire, a conjurer gives the utmost respect, admiration, and caution. A wise conjurer studies fire, its flares, its colors, its dance. Using fire for personal benefit is an ambitious, even foolhardy undertaking. Calling fire into being must be deeply considered, with all other avenues examined and rejected first.

This fire is prized for its golden tone, and arsenic is responsible for that. Arsenic comes from the Syric word for yellow. Acquire Moroccan arsenic for the best, deepest color flames.

This fire is a cleansing fire. The addition of boron, discovered by the Seven Sisters, empowers its flames to sear away the past and disintegrate taints and flaws. The effects of this fire are utterly irreversible.

Again the reader is cautioned against creating fire. Cobalt is another reason for caution! Not for nothing was this element named by the Germans for their word for goblin: kobold. The fire summoned here will not be reliably controlled. Take note.

This fire has been designed to withstand quelling attempts by other conjurers' methods. It is tantalum's extremely high melting and boiling points and ability to fend off acid's corrosive destruction which render this fire's strength formidable.

Air

The very invisibility of air makes it the most intriguing of the four classical elements, while the density of thin air works beautifully to a conjurer's purposes. Air's very transparency offers infinite hiding places for spells, incantations, snippets of information, secrets, and de-configured objects. Air will be found to be full to any eye but the naïve, unschooled eye, for the air around us teems with data, with signals, with communications from spirits, to and from conjurers, alive and dead.

This mixture's secret ingredient: Einsteinium. Contemporary readers will wonder at this ingredient, an element from the future, created from an unimaginable event, an event both destructive and creative.

Iron links this air with the earth and makes it more manageable. The ancient connection and complicated dance between air and iron add to the balanced and stable nature of this alchemical air.

On the other hand, the lightest element and the lightest metal, lithium always flirts with air. Here they are brought into wholeness to use their gifts together in a floating, transparent, yet strong and supple, power. Tennessine is chosen for its location in "the island of stability," a place of chemical contradictions.

A note about vanadium: this element has in the past been known by another name, discovered by a conjurer in an atomic conjuring feat of sparks and fire. His discovery was deemed sorcery, not science, a useless distinction! The name was changed based on this spurious objection to his processes.

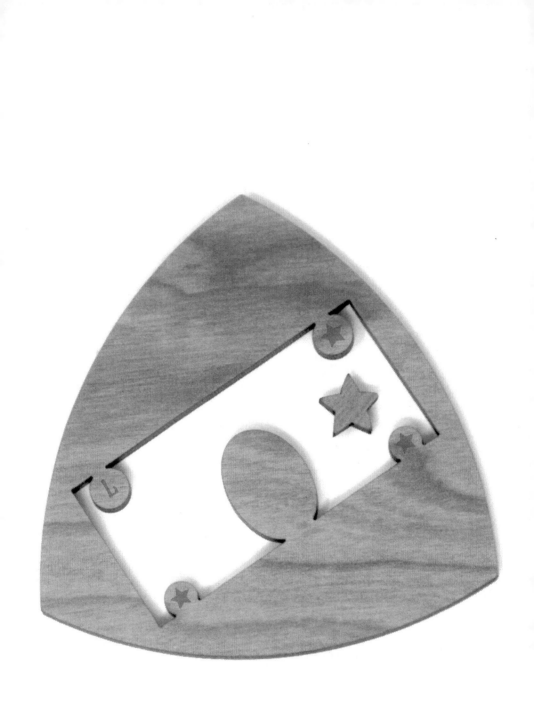

Money

For those readers who have turned directly to this page driven by the delusion that it is only necessary to create money and, from that, all other substances will be attainable, cease! Desist! Not even considering the issue of the seven deadly sins, there are better paths to follow when seeking only money as the reward. Abandon the path of conjuring immediately!

For those who will bring forth money as a tool, such will find that this alchemical lucre shifts easily in form to distract and conquer the greedy. Malleability of remuneration, a highly desirable characteristic, is provided by aluminum.

Argon, an inexpensive, common, and inactive element, enhances the easily exchangeable and transferrable characteristics of the money resulting from these instructions.

Finally, add yttrium to money to make use of the element's superconductivity, and, perhaps somewhat ironically, its curative properties.

The student of conjuring must be warned that the money created here will come to emit an unpleasant odor, undetectable at the time of exchange. This is due to the sulfur in it. Therefore, it should not be created to be hoarded.

Psychokinesis

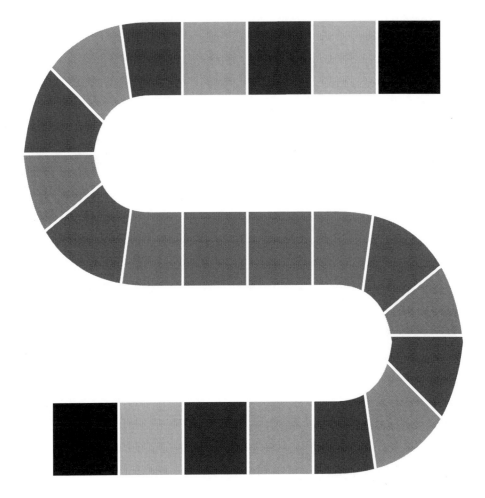

Legend has it that some people have the power of "mind over matter," a paranormal ability to move inanimate objects through space and time. Hogwash! Any conjurer can learn psychokinesis with enough practice!

Mind over Truth

The term "mind over matter," however, is not completely inaccurate. The secret of psychokinesis lies in convincing an object that it is not what, where, or when it thinks it is. Illusions become reality; truth becomes malleable, not what it was before.

After a series of unfortunate accidents, practitioners of psychokinesis have come up with some important safety rules to prevent future problems. Following these rules will help prevent tragedies like accelerating a pool ball to the speed of light and having it end up inside a person.

Every movement must move an object to a real world *venue* known by the conjurer, so that the conjurer can picture the venue well. Initial venues are combined to make more venues. If one of these venues is mistakenly a fictional venue, it must not be used.

A skilled conjurer always has a final goal clearly in mind. When everything but the final goal has been achieved, and not earlier, two-letter abbreviations of venues are used to help with focus. (If a venue does not have a standard two-letter abbreviation, conjurers use the first two letters.)

Finally, but critically, when an object is moved into the future, it is reversed, as if seen in a mirror. Because of this, any movement to the future must be paired with a reversal spell.

Beginning conjurers should start with well-known places and times. Picturing a goal accurately while repeating its associated numerical chant is the key to reaching it. Each of the following pages provides a list of optimal places and times for practicing psychokinesis.

Yesterday

While psychokinesis can be used to move objects to any time in the past, it is prudent to attempt closer times first. These venues move the object to the same spot and the same hour of the day, but the previous day.

Restaurant and arcade chain founded by a co-founder of Atari
Hyatt, Hilton, or Holiday Inn
Grassy area past the bases
French city which The Big Easy is indirectly named after
Oval racing track like the one near Indianapolis
When people go to the ballot box
You could get lost in the pages of one for 10¢, back when a pound
of steak also cost 10¢
Home of the Los Angeles Forum
Egyptian location of a famous ancient library
Town in England whose Earl is in *King Lear*
Orchard with certain citrus fruits

5 1. 6'1, 5, 8, 7, 8, 8 3, 4 5, 9, 10, 10, 6 5

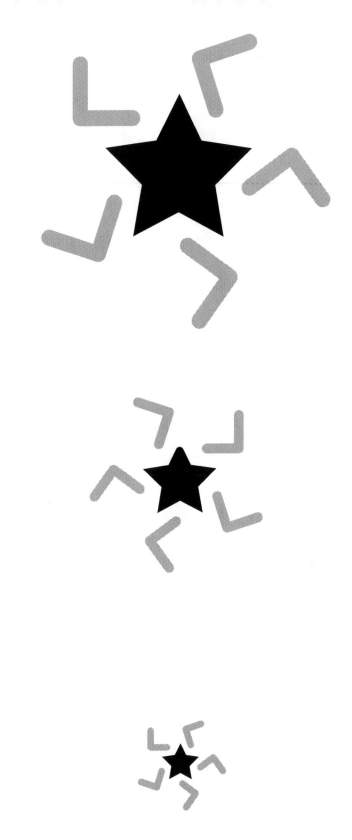

Seconds Ago

It might seem that moving something mere seconds into the past is a lot less useful than moving it far in the past. Conjuring wisdom has taught us that it is best to go back only as far as necessary. Besides, in many cases, just a few seconds is enough time to redeem a catastrophic mistake!

Only country with a national flag that isn't a quadrilateral shape
An eagle's nest
A maze
Where Bilbo lived
End of the workweek
New York birthplace of Kodak and Xerox
Ship full of crude stuff
Dormant volcano which is supposedly where Noah's Ark landed

5, 5, 9, 5, 6, 9, 3 6, 5 6

Up

Moving objects up a little effectively makes them lighter, while moving objects up a lot allows you to move them long distances without significant effort. With this psychokinetic effect, we suspect ancient conjurers aided the construction of not a few temples, and at least one Central American pyramid.

It's held every two years, alternating Summer and Winter
Where the self-important lawyers work in *Better Call Saul*
"Lovely" asteroid visited by a space probe in 1998, and one of the
    first sites of human colonization in *The Expanse*
Place for a pint while watching the Kansas Jayhawks or the
    World Cup
Tallinn is its capital
Tax day in the US, usually
Forty-seventh state to join the United States of America
Country from 1955 to 1975 that had its capital in Saigon
December Twenty-first, roughly
Place where students could find all the world's knowledge, before
    the world wide web existed
Place where plays are usually produced in alternation or rotation,
    sometimes with the same actors in multiple productions
Home of perhaps the most famous opera house in the world
Constellation between Aries the Ram and Gemini the Twins
Eight-hundred-year anniversary

3 9, 3, 4, 6 3, 7, 5 9, 3 6, 5 7, 6 8, 12, 9 7, 6 9, 6 3 4, 14

Down

Moving objects down with psychokinesis can make them heavier. But if they are moved down just the right amount, they can become, effectively, immovable. A Tibetan story tells of a conjurer using this technique to anchor an urn, which in turn held a rope over a cliff to help monks escape murderous marauders! This technique can block paths and entryways, produce obstructions for pursuers to trip over, protect light objects from being blown away. It is quite useful!

State where Mount Holyoke College is located
Early place in cyberspace, once part of Time-Warner
Pacific Island nation which was the first to see the third millennium
Where the train stops to go back
Massachusetts town used by cruciverbalists as the name for an
    unfair crossing in a crossword
Unoccupied spot at the table
1969 rock festival with a comic strip character named after it

13,   3,   8,   3 2 3 4,   6,   5 5,   9

+ 5 1 6 5 3 6 1

+ 0 0 0 4 9 7 2

K E Y H O L E

Push

Pushing an object is most frequently used as a defensive maneuver, like deflecting a weapon or causing an opponent to fall when something is pushed in front of them. The push resulting from this psychokinetic technique may function more like a strong shove, but the more experienced conjurers add remarkable finesse and subtlety. They are able to produce slight nudges that can influence outcomes in remarkable ways!

Surprisingly, maple syrup represents only $1/10\%$ of its total
   economic activity
Northern California river named after Pacific lamprey that never
   swam there
Canadian territory that has less than 39,000 people in an area of
   1,877,787 km² (that's about 48 km² per person)
The one third of Michigan that is connected by land to Wisconsin
   but not the rest of Michigan
Area that became the German Democratic Republic in 1949
Largest city in Brazil
Major galaxy that is the closest to us
Where one might dissect a frog
Birthplace of Miró

7, 3, 7, 5 9, 4 4, 3 5, 9, 7 3, 9

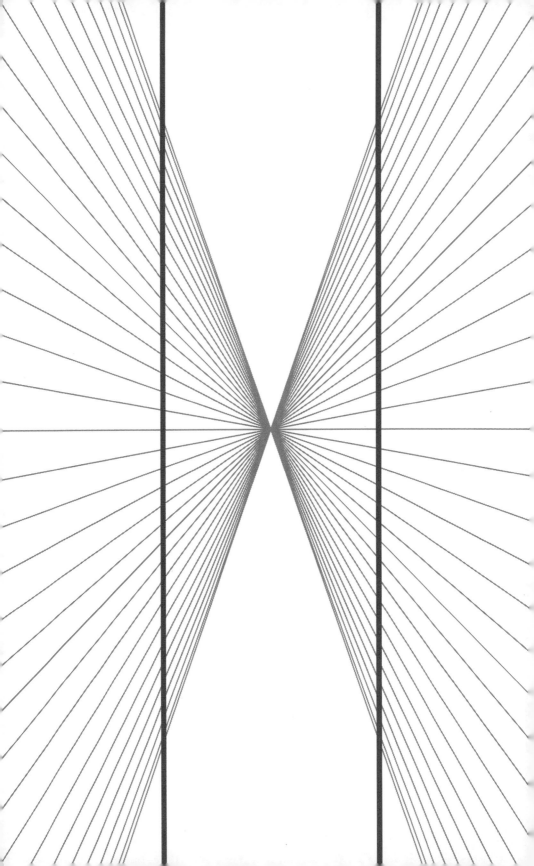

Pull

The most common use of pulling is to pick up things quickly, but it is more useful for pulling things out of balance and making them collapse. As with the previous technique, pulling will first be more similar to yanking, but, with practice, the pull can be so slight as to feel to the subject as if they are making the decision to go a certain direction themselves.

City that has a country inside it
Place to meet people online, a competitor to Cupid and OkCupid
First group in a string orchestra
Place for apps that comes in 7.9″, 9.7″, 10.5″, and 12.9″ sizes
Place to live that anagrams to something you might build a place
    to live out of
Former Soviet Socialist Republic whose capital is Dushanbe
Their flag is almost identical to Monaco's (a red horizontal band
    above a white one)
Site of a famous 1881 gunfight featuring Wyatt, Virgil, and
    Morgan Earp, plus Doc Holliday
Managua's country
Their flag has a white equilateral cross on a red field
Annual celebration of sorts when people play practical jokes on
    one another

4, 8, 6 7, 4, 5, 10, 9, 1.1. 6, 9, 11, 5 5' 3

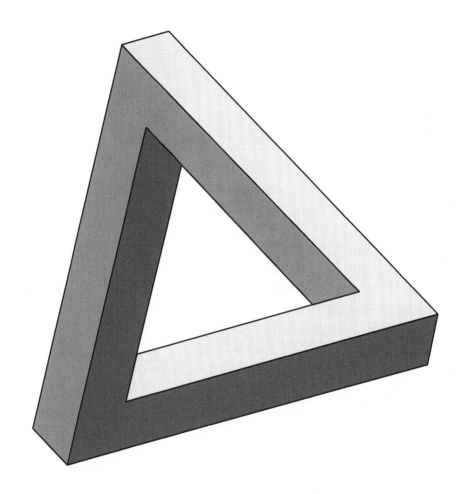

Seconds from Now

To someone who doesn't know psychokinesis, moving something a few seconds into the future has the effect of making something vanish and then reappear. If it's not a timepiece of some sort, there's little difference. Repeated carefully, the vanishing effect can be quite striking, without any danger of permanently losing the object!

Companion to Burger King and Jack in the Box?
Irish capital
Los Angeles institution whose mascot is not a Trojan warrior but a white horse
Street named in the *Green Acres* theme
Phantom passageway written about by Norton Juster
Undersea hideaway sung about by The Beatles
Largest US state by population
Traveling show that merged with Barnum & Bailey in 1919 to become "The Greatest Show on Earth"

5 5, 6, 3, 4 6, 9, 7'1 6, 10, 8 8 6

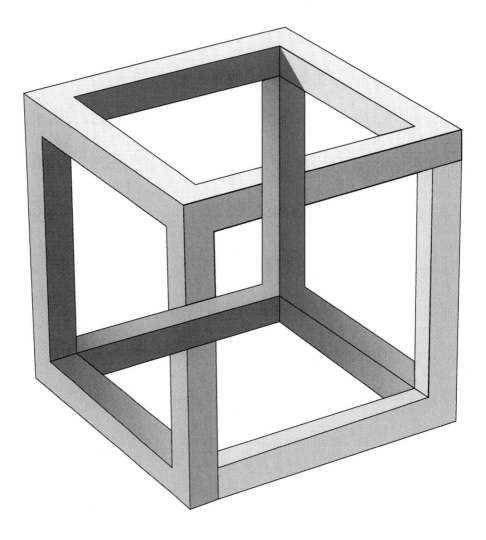

Tomorrow

Moving anything into the far future is both difficult and dangerous. At best, the future is unpredictable; at worst, it is predictable in ways that are not desired. Conjurers must take special care to only move objects to future times and locations which can be well controlled to avoid problems!

Worldwide celebration on April twenty-second
Site of the first modern Olympic games
Capital of Iran
It was the tallest in the world for forty years
It's fed by the Mississippi and the Rio Grande
Any one of Jupiter, Saturn, Uranus, or Neptune (but not
    Pluto anymore)
Underwater city
Los Angeles neighborhood with a 2002 film named after it

5 3, 6, 6, 6 5 8, 4 2 6, 5 6, 8, 6 6

Geomancy

In geomancy, conjurers harness the power of the earth's magnetism to great effect. Geomancy harnesses the innate magnetism of all the metals which are spread throughout the soil and water.

Geomancy Families

 There are many different families of geomancy, each with its own powers and limitations. For reasons unknown, geomancy families tend to come in geographical clusters of four locations that define a quadrilateral.

Conjurers love to fly, and flying is one of the biggest benefits of learning Geomancy. As a result, advanced conjurers do not need airplanes.

However, beginning conjurers generally travel via more traditional means, only visiting cities with airports. As a result, they become rather well acquainted with flying centers, from famous centers like SFO to small, less well-known centers like AZO.

Things have changed greatly since the days when conjurers learning about geomancy had to travel by hot air balloon. Today, there are airports all over the world, even in the middle of the ocean. Some small islands even have more than one airport from which to choose.

There is a peculiarity to geomancy, one that brings a smile to the face of many a conjurer. When geomancy was first discovered, the Earth was flat, or at least that was so believed. Today, of course, we know the Earth is shaped like a sphere. Yet, geomancy works better when conjurers, at least temporarily, embrace the concept that the Earth is flat (or at least more flat). It's a bit tough to do, but the difference in results is astounding!

Wellington
Christchurch
Timaru
Dunedin
Chatham I.
(N.Z.)
Bounty Trough
Pitt I.
Bounty I.
(N. Z.)
Antipodes Is.
Auckland-Is.
(N.Z.)
Campbell-I.

Soil

Conjurers suspected that the soil around a city could be a boon to geomancy. It is not the elements in the soil *per se*, but the ratio of those elements, conjurers have learned, and those proportions must be measured with precision. The soil of Maracaibo, Venezuela was the first one that revealed that its soil gave geomancy more power.

Identifying the geoactivity of soil generally requires a portable laboratory. Gaining access to geomancy's power through soil necessitates detailed understanding of the metals present and their proportions. The ancient laboratory equipment used to identify the intense geoactivity of the soil of La Paz, Bolivia and Pucallpa, Peru was heavy, fragile, and volatile. By modern standards, it is amazing that the testing was even accomplished. Every conjurer will need distilled water, the *sine qua non* of soil testing. Beyond that, conjurers develop their own preferred laboratory methods over time, which these days can be fairly compact. The great mystic Quenzujavier has developed the most compact and efficient portable soil-testing laboratory to date. Please refer to his work *Tierra* for an exploration of methods and equipment.

Relatively recently, another conjurer identified the power of Georgetown, Guyana, the most powerful soil location known today, but he has not yet, and contrary to custom in the conjuring community, shared his methods. Therefore, his name will be withheld from this volume.

Water

Water in the air responds to the earth's magnetic forces, just as seawater and the water in human bodies do. Certain locations respond in specific, magnetic ways to levels of humidity in the air, making them highly geoactive.

Expert conjurers are able to judge the humidity content without instruments, but have quite varied methods for doing so. Three examples follow:

First is the method that led to the discovery of Qaqortoq, Greenland and Havana, Cuba. Estimating the humidity in the air within a tenth of a percentage point can be accomplished by observing a thin strip of rice paper held in the palm of the hand.

Francisco the Magnificent, who was the first to identify both Munich, Germany and Greenville, Liberia, can judge humidity levels with similar accuracy, though less consistently, by an itching or lack thereof around the beds of his fingernails. (Once, the sensation occurred in his toenails, but that has not been repeated.)

Finally, it is said that another conjurer uses a vessel of water and reads its ripples, while another sees shifts in the face of the moon depending on humidity. The aspiring conjurer would do well to cultivate a calibration method for measuring a location's humidity level as well!

Flora

The plants that spring from the earth manifest its metals in every leaf and frond. Unusual flora in a region can make it a geoactivity goldmine, so to speak.

Orchids on New Britain, Papua New Guinea, attract magnetic pull through the shape of their petals. Some argue that this is actually caused by the ants colonizing their roots, but this volume will not undertake that argument.

The screwpine (or *pandanus fanning enosis*) in Bairiki, Kiribati, seems to form a sort of basket or (for future readers) a satellite dish for magnetic waves. Conjurers have not determined whether it is the shape or the texture of screwpine leaves that give them this effect.

The flora on Airlie Beach, Australia and other nearby islands is so rich and varied that conjurers have not been able to identify the specific ones that create the effect of geomancy. Many suspect that the octopus bushes are the source, but credible assertions have been made about the coastal she-oak and the hoop pines.

The Tahitian gardenias on Koro Island, Fiji are the reason for its geomancy feasibility. It is generally believed that these flowers create geomancy conditions because of the tubular nature of their petals. It was originally thought that it was the aroma of the Tahitian gardenias that was the cause, but this was preposterous and has been disproven definitively!

Aroma

Areas of the world sometimes have a geomagnetic aroma. This is not an aroma that can be discerned by the untrained nose. Nevertheless, here is an attempt to describe what conjurers report smelling in the key locations of this family.

In Sofia, Bulgaria, the smell was something akin to what one would smell if a container of oregano were opened across the room. The smell was subtle and green. As with all of the aroma family, an image arrives in the conjurer's mind along with the odor. In this case the image was of a wrought-iron gate. The assumption is that the nose recognized a connection to iron and magnetism that was undiscoverable through other senses.

In Kiev, Ukraine, conjurers can smell a strong jasmine aroma. In some places, it can be strong enough to be somewhat intoxicating! The aroma is present even during winter, when there is no chance that is from a tropical flower, and it would be highly unlikely at any time in that region!

The aromas in Kabul, Afghanistan and Baghdad, Iraq are both more like perfume than natural substances. Kabul's aroma has been described as *eau de cologne*, while Baghdad's aroma is reported to smell surprisingly similar to the product known as Shalimar.

Vision

Like people, places on earth radiate visible auras. Unlike people, the aura of a place can be hard to see, even by specialists. As a result, many conjurers doubted the existence of visible location auras until 1807, when an objective conjurer, Meghan the Mage, had the great good fortune to inhabit the body of the late lamented Psyche the Powerful.

The two conjurers had embarked on an endeavor to search out geomancy families. Since aeroplanes were not part of the common modes of travel at the time, and no geoactive locations were convenient to their needs, they resorted to the corporal transfer method (this volume does not include this technique for obvious reasons of necessary skill level). They needed Psyche to see the auras of cities where Meghan's body was, and Meghan to classify the essence of the cities where Psyche's body was. While in each other's bodies, they were able to bring their own discriminating abilities, but much to their surprise, they were also able to perceive that which the host body perceived. Thus, Meghan realized that visible auras were indeed extant and perceivable, and the result was the co-discovery of Thimpu, Bhutan and Changsha, China.

Later, a conjurer's collective was created to search for additional locations, resulting in the discovery and confirmation of the powers of Bangkok, Thailand and Manila, Philippines.

AMRITSAR
Chandigarh
DELHI
NEW DELHI
Jodhpur
Luni R.
Ajmer
Aligarh
Mathura
Agra
JAIPUR
GWALIOR
Jhansi
Ujjain
Betwa R.
Narmada R.
JABALPUR
KANPUR
ALLAHABAD
Varanasi
PATNA
Bhagalpur
Ranchi
Asansol
JAMSHEDPUR
Bhatpara
HAORA
CALCUTTA
Khulna
CHITTAGONG
Cuttack
Raipur
Nagpur
Akola
Aurangabad
Nanded
Warangal
HYDERABAD
Vijayawada
Guntur
Kakinada
Machilipatnam (Bandar)
Nellore
MADRAS
N
D
I
A
Bay of
Bengal
Ramree I.
Cheduba I.

Electricity

Some facts are known to conjurers, but not to the public at large. This is one of them: cities can generate electricity — not very much, but enough to register on the measuring devices used for conjuring purposes. A conjurer does not look for enough electricity to light up houses or spin a merry-go-round. No. A conjurer looks only for a spark to use for their purposes.

Ocean City, Maryland is one such place. In every language, profession, relationship, there are some things that just are. If one asks "why?" one receives the answer, "It just is." That is how it is with this situation. This is the truest answer for the reason any of these cities can be used for geomancy.

In contrast, some have speculated that the electricity generated by Central Park in New York City is merely a reflection of city lights on the ponds. The industrial activity in Hershey, Pennsylvania has been cited as a possible source of its special electrical spark. And, in Newport News, Virginia, guesses have been made regarding the historic battles fought nearby and their lasting effects. Yet, in each case, definitive documentary evidence exists showing sparks dating back to the 1600s, before any of these alternative explanations could have been possible.

It bears repeating that the best answer to "why?" in this case remains: "It just is."

Stars

Every inhabited place on Earth has a constellation affinity, a position in the sky that corresponds with favorable conditions in that location. But some locations have a super affinity, which makes conjuring almost effortless.

For tens of thousands of years it has been known that Quito, Ecuador flourishes under *Kaza Maiyaya*, the Hen with Chickens constellation named by the African Hausa people. This was known so early because Quito is incredibly geoactive, and it could be argued that the ancients understood stars better than scholars do now. In fact, all of the most powerful locations for this family were discovered quite early.

In 1533, Incan astronomer Elonanahui discovered the super affinity of Colider, Brazil with *Atoq*, the Incan fox constellation. His cousin, the conjurer we know today as Huiuoatl, consulted with Elonanahui to discover that Paramibo, Suriname had a super affinity with *Hanp'atu*, the Toad constellation. Huaraz, Peru has an affinity with *Mach'acuay*, the Serpent, a fact that was shared with the world by a Peruvian conjurer.

It is generally believed that many more super affinity sites for constellations exist since the possibilities are, though not infinite, certainly as numerous as there are cities on Earth. Perhaps readers of this Almanaq will discover more such locations!

.

Sounds

Locations in this family have a particular sound, and that sound is akin to the music of the spheres as described by Pythagoras to the pharaohs. Today, his claim that he could hear the movement of the spheres is considered to be metaphorical. Yet, Pythagoras sent conjurers clues through his writings, teaching them how to listen for the celestial harmonies he perceived.

The sound in Ottawa, Canada can be heard only in late winter between midnight and dawn. Those who have heard it consider themselves very lucky, because it is both powerful and pleasurable, calling to mind the sound of blood coursing through the human body with every heartbeat. Ottawa is also the home of one of the greats of musical conjuring, Maestra Majicali, who holds lectures and classes on the subject once or twice a century. Readers who are interested in pursuing this subject should make every effort to attend the next time she is teaching.

Maracaibo, Venezuela's sound is perhaps the easiest to hear, as regular people, not just conjurers, have been known to perceive the deep groan without knowing what it could be. All describe it as the sound of something important on its way here.

London, England's version of the music of the spheres is described by a majority of conjurers who have heard it as a sound one hears through one's feet. The sound of Gibraltar, on the other hand, comes, they say, as if one is hearing it through one's spine.

Incantations

Wynken, Blynken, and Nod one night, sailed off in a wooden shoe, sailed on a river of crystal light into a sea of dew. "Where are you going, and what do you wish?" the old moon asked the three.

"We have come to fish
for the herring-fish
that live in this beautiful sea;
nets of silver and gold have we,"
Said Wynken, Blynken, and Nod.

The old moon laughed and sang a song, as they rocked in the wooden shoe; and the wind that sped them all night long ruffled the waves of dew; the little stars were the herring-fish that lived in the beautiful sea.

"Now cast your nets
wherever you wish,
Never afraid are we!"
So cried the stars
to the fishermen three.

All night long their nets they threw to the stars in the twinkling foam; then down from the skies came the wooden shoe, bringing the fishermen home: 'twas all so pretty a sail, it seemed as if it could not be; and some folk thought 'twas a dream they'd dreamed of sailing that beautiful sea.

Eugene Field

Easiest of all the ancient conjuring arts is the art of incantations, a veritable panoply of passion and poetry. Therefore, many an essential guidebook starts with them. But with ease comes risk, not safety, and that is why they are near the end of this Almanaq.

The Magic of Poetry

 As poets talk about the "magic" of poetry, they are conveying the power of words, meter, verse, rhymes, rhythm and even lines of poetry to set a mood, or to offer a feeling. If poets knew that their words truly had special powers, they would be shocked!

Though it is true that all incantations are poems, not all poems are incantations. There is no encyclopedia of incantations, no list to be consulted for the incredible things that may be done through serious incantation.

Trained conjurers will learn to recognize incantations where they live, without having to examine every single line of prose they encounter. Like the symbol stones hidden throughout the world, incantations hide in plain sight. While incantations may, of course, be read aloud with appropriately serious tone and timbre, it is not keenly required. Conjurers will learn to appreciate the work it takes to create a proper incantation, getting the mood, feel, and even lines just right.

Do not modify a poem written by others to change its power or to turn a regular poem into an incantation. (Those presented here are the originals.) In a similar vein, only true masters of incantations have the wherewithal to understand fully and wield properly the poetic powers of meter, rhyme, alliteration, and even acrostics in creating incantations. If the choice of phrasing is slightly odd or has uneven lines, an incantation will fail or, much worse, yield a sudden catastrophic result. Nobody wants to get blamed for the next Krakatoa!

What is pink? a rose is pink
By a fountain's brink.
What is red? a poppy's red
In its barley bed.
What is blue? the sky is blue
Where the clouds float thro'.
What is white? a swan is white
Sailing in the light.
What is yellow? pears are yellow,
Rich and ripe and mellow.
What is green? the grass is green,
With small flowers between.
What is violet? clouds are violet
In the summer twilight.
What is orange? Why, an orange,
Just an orange!

Christina Rossetti

Colors

An incantation of colors can be dismissed as worthless, not of significance for anything. After all, what is color but an outward appearance, a single aspect of an object. That's true, but the truth is more complicated.

In the real world of conjuring as well as fictional poetic places like Xanadu, appearances matter. And, of all the things that eyes can perceive, color is the most important, far more important than texture or tone.

The incantations of color are the beginning. Complete control of hues and tints is the key to everything that follows in the art of incantations — effortless transformation of colors will unlock the power of a million incantations.

Fall, leaves, fall; die, flowers, away;
Lengthen night and shorten day;
Every leaf speaks bliss to me
Fluttering from the autumn tree.
I shall smile when wreaths of snow
Blossom where the rose should grow;
I shall sing when night's decay
Ushers in a drearier day.

Emily Brontë

Weather

It is not surprising that a poem about weather functions well as not only a poem but also as an incantation. Weather has been used by artists in all media as a metaphor for interior landscapes, for emotions that cannot be described effectively without vivid visual imagery. And everyone knows how much weather can affect moods!

Some conjurers will seek to alter the weather as a way to make a fortune selling emergency supplies after flooding, materials for reinforcing houses before hurricanes, and even tools for snow and ice removal. Regretfully, all four examples listed here have been used by conjurers. But, ethical conjurers will not use incantations for personal gain. This is especially important with something as powerful as the weather. Misuse of such elemental forces has been the basis of many a disaster.

Oh, come to me in dreams, my love!
I will not ask a dearer bliss;
Come with the starry beams, my love,
And press mine eyelids with thy kiss.

'Twas thus, as ancient fables tell,
Love visited a Grecian maid,
Till she disturbed the sacred spell,
And woke to find her hopes betrayed.

But gentle sleep shall veil my sight,
And Psyche's lamp shall darkling be,
When, in the visions of the night,
Thou dost renew thy vows to me.

Then come to me in dreams, my love,
I will not ask a dearer bliss;
Come with the starry beams, my love,
And press mine eyelids with thy kiss.

Mary Wollstonecraft Shelley

Dreams

The realm of sleep contains its own conjuring. In sleep, the mind has its mastery of the conjurer's skills, causing images, sensations, and emotions to become vividly real to the sleeping person. The lax mind at sleep is a vulnerable subject, one not fully understood by any profession, from doctor to artist to salesman to conjurer. In the realm of Queen Mab, humans can only dabble, playing around the edges to inject tiny influences into the vast, unplumbed nuances of the unconscious.

Incantations can affect a sleeping mind with small but important effects. Like an alarm clock, an incantation can be brought into the sleeping mind. How exactly the human mind will do this and for what purpose cannot be completely controlled. Conjurers throughout time, particularly the academicians, have tried to identify the causes and actions, to no success. In the meantime, take care and use caution. Be prepared for unexpected results!

I see it as it looked one afternoon
In August, — by a fresh soft breeze o'erblown.
The swiftness of the tide, the light thereon,
A far-off sail, white as a crescent moon.
The shining waters with pale currents strewn,
The quiet fishing-smacks, the Eastern cove,
The semi-circle of its dark, green grove.
The luminous grasses, and the merry sun
In the grave sky; the sparkle far and wide,
Laughter of unseen children, cheerful chirp
Of crickets, and low lisp of rippling tide,
Light summer clouds fantastical as sleep
Changing unnoted while I gazed thereon.
All these fair sounds and sights
       I made my own.

Emma Lazarus

Sensation

As poets know, sensations reveal the world to us in nonverbal ways, for our minds can react to them without our knowledge. Lazarus's poem evokes a range of sensations, and our minds can recreate those sensations. That is the power of this incantation, allowing a conjurer to cause the subject's mind to perceive sensory input that hasn't occurred in the physical realm.

A particularly effective sensation is touch, in the form of a tap on a wrist or shoulder. The subject can be distracted from almost any task or point of focus with the feeling that someone is touching or nudging them to get their attention.

Another sensation that can be very distracting is that of an insect racing somewhere on the body, especially if it seems to be a spider. Reactions range from frantic brushing, to yelping, to shaking dances. All of these reactions can be leveraged, but it must be noted that the extent of a human's fear of spiders defies prediction!

"Hope" is the thing with feathers
That perches in the soul
And sings the tune without the words
And never stops at all

And sweetest in the gale is heard
And sore must be the storm
That could abash the little bird
That kept so many warm

I've heard it in the chillest land
And on the strangest sea
Yet, never, in Extremity,
It asked a crumb of me.

Emily Dickinson

Flight

Since the age of dinosaurs there has been an absolute fact: *flying needs feathers* (although featherless squirrels may seem to fly, they are really falling slowly). Therefore, feathers are the focus of this flight incantation, aiming for an organic manifestation of our feathered friends' enviable capability. Internalizing this is the secret to flight.

Nothing is as light as a feather — it has as much air as matter — and this is crucial to using this incantation. The conjurer must think about both the feather and the air within it in order to exercise the power of flight smoothly and without mishap.

Human flight has been a desire since the dawn of humanity, so it is no surprise that incantations have existed for centuries. Dickinson's poetic masterpiece is merely the latest and most controllable incarnation, now available to even beginning conjurers.

This is the debt I pay
Just for one riotous day,
Years of regret and grief,
Sorrow without relief.

Pay it I will to the end —
Until the grave, my friend,
Gives me a true release —
Gives me the clasp of peace.

Slight was the thing I bought,
Small was the debt I thought,
Poor was the loan at best —
God! but the interest!

Paul Laurence Dunbar

Money

It should come as no surprise that conjuring wealth was one of the original intents of conjuring, which is one reason why there are so many ways to make money. It seems, so often, to be the simple explanation to a problem, and, indeed, it can be. But with so many other solutions at a conjurer's disposal, it is advisable to settle on money only after having considered, carefully and thoroughly, the many alternatives.

For this incantation, one cannot expect it will produce money that is magically free from obligation. In fact, money produced by this incantation *always* comes with strings attached, sometimes very unexpected strings, which can have an impact that is impossible to foresee.

Even in conjuring, old adages can apply — money doesn't grow on trees.

Very soon the Yankee teachers
   Came down and set up school;
But, oh! how the Rebs did hate it, —
   It was agin' their rule.

Our masters always tried to hide
   Book learning from our eyes;
Knowledge didn't agree with slavery —
   'Twould make us all too wise.

But some of us would try to steal
   A little from the book.
And put the words together,
   And learn by hook or crook.

Frances Ellen Watkins Harper

Knowledge

This incantation summons very particular knowledge evoked by Harper's poem: knowledge wrongfully withheld. This incantation will not work as a workaround for mindreading. Despite this limitation, however, this incantation is quite useful.

Importantly, this incantation is extremely sensitive to the conjurer's intent in discovering the knowledge sought. It will lock knowledge away more tightly if the conjurer is looking for a way to get a numerical advantage in order satisfy a greedy impulse. This may be hard to believe, but trust that this incantation will divine the existential difference between a plan to plunder and an intent to rob the rich to give to the poor.

For such infractions, there are conjurers who have lost the use of this incantation permanently. Conjurers should always take care to only use this incantation with the purest of intentions!

Youth, large, lusty, loving —
youth full of grace, force, fascination,

Do you know that Old Age
may come after you
with equal grace, force, fascination?

Day full-blown and splendid —
day of the immense sun,
action, ambition, laughter,

The Night follows close
with millions of suns,
and sleep and restoring darkness.

Walt Whitman

Time

This is an incantation that can turn back time. Yes, conjurers can use this incantation to manipulate time! Of course, as with other techniques described in this volume, this one has some significant restrictions. The meddling that can be done with time with this incantation goes one way: backward.

That is the first caveat. The second is that the whole of the time must be relived. One conjurer went back in time to bet on a horse race. He was richly rewarded, but, by the time he lived through the intervening years back to the present, all of his winnings had been spent — every last cent was gone, and he was worse off in many ways than when he had started.

Other ways of manipulating time have different restrictions and caveats, so it is important to consider both the purpose and the restrictions when contemplating a time-manipulating activity. Many a conjurer has had what started as a quick time jaunt end in disaster, all due to the lack of advance preparation.

Displacement

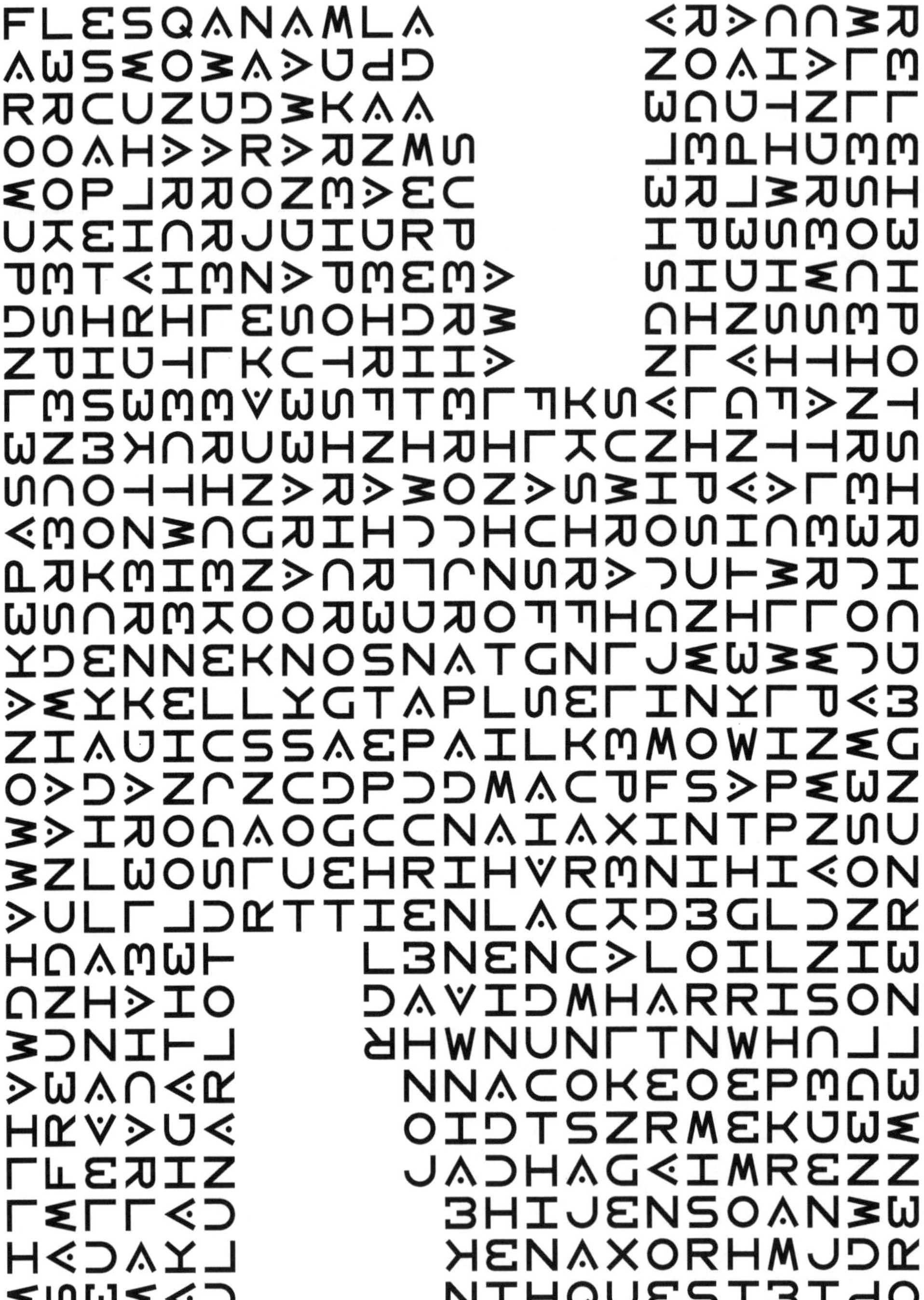

Some people describe displacement as human psychokinesis, in which conjurers move themselves, rather than inanimate objects, through space and time. But, in reality, everything is different.

Displacement Matrixes

 Conjurers almost always plan an entire itinerary of displacements together, using a series of displacement matrixes that allow them to coordinate all of their movements together.

Displacement matrixes use the special **WIM** alphabet designed to make them hard for laypeople to understand. *Even conjurers need to read carefully in order to avoid misreading letters!*

ΛƐⅭↃƐ𝖥Ꮐ𝖧ⅠꞀ𝖪Ⅼ𝖬𝖭ᴑ𝖯ᴑᴙꙄ𝖳ᴜ𝗏𝗪᙭ʏⵣ

Itinerary planning starts with *Small Matrixes*. In each Small Matrix, the conjurer must eliminate everything distracting from the destination, leaving an essential pair of letters. Distractors are always horizontal or vertical, but may run in any direction.

Next, the conjurer moves on to an *Empty Matrix* like the one shown at right, with one column for each Small Matrix (this example would be appropriate were one to have four Small Matrixes). Each pair, in the order the letters are given, fills in a single column of the Empty Matrix. It is only at this stage that the conjurer can determine the sequence of destinations in order to get the proper directions.

The conjurer next turns to the *Large Matrixes*. Using the directions gleaned from the Empty Matrix, the conjurer extracts further instructions *(orientation matters!)* from all the Large Matrixes which allows them to determine their final path.

Some new conjurers confuse matrixes with latitude and longitude. *They are not the same!* While such "GPS" coordinates may be useful for other conjuring purposes, they are useless for displacement.

PUCXUAEDSONAEKACANDYHAT
OAHQIIROTRRICLAJNYNHILH
HTURVYEAMUPAOMODRARUMG
SRIIHTSLNP3CNROHOHRYCNI
IWSLUVOCLWLANEUNRT&<ZEN
EURT-RNMECOMASCGZAEJAMK
GZ3EHINYYCCEOEUTGKKHMOE
GHKRMWIMDMNRJONESAAUONH
OUNPMPTM>UIICFNU>PJHZIT
THOEUPTAC>VAM3IAEONOWCE
TWTR-3ATNPELTRDCLSWD>SR
NAGSMAUDWUKCWUAKTVWUUSA
EWST<UTTUTOHTTM<HIMITIL
GT3AMIOCC U5EMH>MEF
A<TLURZU TNRMPRHS
TZP3ZH>K UOEK3IEC
EORYNUTJ 4UAHHATO
RXMROZIEK URNLWV3AT
CHUHTW>NSAD NNDTPISZRNT
EU>UWAZNKWANAIP3RTLLIOW
STMTEWUIORPVIKW3OY3NASW
W>RK3OCFNWRTCPRNJ3P3NRU
ORU<SAREAYAVIW>1EEHIPEU
JUTZAW-RSWHPTUHNCNVTLT>
JZRAFHHLOHEOSTJ6TDNVETR
W>OREUUCOJIDIVJTNEI3TAR
FXWORUACKJGVGN<0ER3SCPH
UMUMD<D>IWNCOIHNIVWTHIU
ZTAUWWZCMRAVLAZJRHO3EK>
O>PWAKNVAVRRTEIVNNHRIT
L1SA<UYR592RKKD3E8KCINO

Flowers

Many a conjurer has planned a displacement around flowers. From visiting the first cherry blossoms around the world to seeing the first blooms across the century, visiting flowers can be peaceful and relaxing. The Hanging Gardens of Babylon, gone now some 2500 years, have been a frequent destination for displacements with a hint of romance.

Of course, some flower displacements have ulterior motives. More than a conjurer or two has profited during the Dutch tulip bubble of the Seventeenth Century. Some are still profiting! There are even rumors that the bubble might have been started by a conjurer, but nobody knows for sure.

```
∀ I L H ∀ ꓷ S ꓴ
H ꓘ ⊢ ɯ ⅃ O H ∀
N Z X O ⅃ I ꓷ ᖴ
N O ⅃ ∀ I ꓴ ꓛ ᖴ
H ɯ < ⊢ I ɯ Ɐ O
N ꓷ S ꓘ ꓵ H Ɐ ꓛ
ꓵ O Z Ꭾ ꓛ H ⅃ H
ꓤ ɯ ꓷ Z ɯ < > ⅃
```

1AZU1PWDJW ALEGALSNWOT
OIAWYSLEKH UERIDSUESS
ZESTYEKYHR ★ PZTUANOREA
EWYLFGRYFFYNEWOFFEJLCWE
RAZUHWAZSSRETTIRNOSAJWE
-PARLISGNASANEEHSSOKED
EUCASOZUREUIWHUIAELSHZN
WHYACLEGUAALUZRAHYKCIRI
AUDREYZWAFFLECLOSETKIMT
PATRICKLICHEONGMANEHGIS
KONIEGATIERFTLAWEWNPRRE
ENWULEHFZESORWAUAKHWEOU
AERNIACKENGOROGNAXWEEQ
FEENKLEKSAWAYWARDREAMER
ELAINEDICKERSONOMLESSAC
HEECRIHPASHTIFFIRGDIVAD
CLPIRATEMILYROSEPUUCIU
UAAHUUOSTAZNOSPEARSONWC
MKIMEEAUAAISNOWWISATEWR
UJOYCEMPSSWCOHNOGONNELL
GPQNSSNHZURNZZHAELZPIWU
LQOUAAIOUSUIOUOLOZHCSUS
MDSGDA UERUSP
FETNDW ZWAAIU
RNULINKCOIZUARLEROWZADP
AEEKPICNHREUELWOWAZLGIN
EWUROEHZWEEYES46EROLYAN
EEZSEYOTSTTODSRASAWURNT
ORSUASZEAZUROTIALULIAUO
OZSZUWEWEHRUWAZEDROEDDR
ELIJAHCJOUREPPHUREPPHLF

Colors

Since the middle ages, all the best artists were conjurers — they were the ones who could obtain the perfect color dyes, those that even today laypeople cannot explain how they were created. The truth, let it be told, is they were created alchemically or by fetching them from the future.

Modern science-based manufacturing techniques have expanded the range of blackest blacks and pinkest pinks that can be produced, making color displacements less necessary for conjurers. Yet, still, there is an allure to displacing to the perfect time and place known for a triple rainbow for inspiration (though some of those places have gotten crowded), or getting a new color dye direct from the source across time!

```
B L U E B O N Y
R A W N Z O R M
I O Z W K U W M
H C N R C B E M
P R W N V K C R
P A I O L B T V
V H R B E W U L
S C A R L E T U
```

FRANK MILLING

MATTHEW STABLE

WALTER

NIGHT

JÖRG MÜLLER

ARDENT

LAHAMLING

HENRY

Sky

Conjurers crave flight, and, with practice, develop facility with it. While flight in earth's atmosphere requires little to no special dress or equipment, visiting the stars is another matter entirely. Conjurers had garb for celestial journeys centuries before NASA and Roscosmos raced to space. These vestments protect and propel the person wearing them with a fabric conjured from feather filaments and wisps of Williwaw wind.

Conjurers travel to the stars partly because they can and partly to gather rare ingredients for conjuring. One conjuring conundrum is how the first helmet for sky displacement came to be, since it is made entirely from material found only among the stars.

AVONASACIMASZAEEERFAZEZ
OZADKJOHNSONUUSRRHXUCCA
NEREEHECAZEOHZEHHAOARAC
ARACHAELFUYSSRGAZZFEENH
IEHCTRONICHKEIRZEZRKADE
LAENEDZGRRTCCUEEHAEAORR
LPROFTOGGUAAHREAZCDURWI
ACUEFISHAEKJRPERTPNNKAG
IRSUEEEDOOHIAOZERAEELH
NOTLIMAHDNITSUJERHXACPT
AJESSICALUCILLERSEEZTOL
MOSAYC ESCEOMD SLPERH
OESESH HAIKMCP TAHRTS
WLIITA PZRAEGE ISDATA
EEEN3E SHNDAOT EEEESE
VIWAVL WROURWE EUOZUI
TGNW3C ZRRIDAR AWYEAH
NFAONI OEAOINT TRLSFT
PTYLRE DIALNHH IAEHME
HKRFAS RUROIAE HRRAAN
PESSMLSIEEORDE3SHSIEAID
PLOO1ALALRNUYNROY♥EMILY
OLMNRKEAKDCELCDV2ELEALR
TEGF3AHSTNURSTPC♦CELHDIH
IYIHZSZGAHRNZZ5ADDESCWU
EHESHAADHWT♦♥♣♠YEOCDUAI
IATYCSAKAYI4H5HEDZUDMSE
HIRNAUYUACSPAMAUSNDJLHR
PAHGEARMAGSPYERROTALHLA
PWOANTHOTKOKEAAAHAYEOZU
OPACTIAHREZHEACZEEUHAAU

Nexus

Sometimes conjurers want to displace themselves to an extremely specific nexus of space and time, where there is no room for error, with possible death being the tragic result of a misstep. This can be difficult when traveling to the past: not only were measurements less precise, but the methods of measurement themselves even varied from place to place.

Therefore, many expert conjurers endeavor to be students of measurement, seeking out arcane and ancient methods from all cultures and eras. They strive to know every measurement from the speed of light to the wavelengths of Krypton-86 to the size of the royal horses in ancient Rome.

Transport

An influential set of conjurers from around the world are strong advocates of the road trip as an invigorating influence on conjurers. They offer a short course, for a fee or barter, to help colleagues determine what kind of road and what kind of vehicle will, shall we say, float their boat.

A surprising number of conjurers find a race on the High Wheeler Penny Farthing to effectively erase the doldrums. Locomotive or caboose rides on one of the many defunct railroads around the world, such as the Cincinnati-Jackson-Mackinaw, does the trick for others. Surprisingly, one of the most popular roads turns out to be a sea road, traveled on a Tongan voyaging kalia.

DEKOLTAEPZJZWJZACMAWAEO
EMERALDATAPWAAARCERMCLD
AENYJIEASWSONCHHCAWAPFS
AGJWZMANILWRTQIAZ EFI
NUEAZPNDTWZEOUAZP ZIG
TMNDMONARYSPIEZUC ZRC
CINLISAVAUGHNLRELLET&HT
NNIECTRIWOPIEILRPCZEGGK
NHNMAEUSIEWUSNDEAE1KL1W
LEGZHREEXTREMEWIREHEADE
HRSMWWILYDIAOSWEAREGOHR
AREOEENSELFSEHUECPPASZE
HMGNENZAIYNUREWWEAVEREC
DAVIDANDREKSOPKELDRINPA
ANAKKSWGSINHWPAILFOOLHK
ZNIEARLHWCNIDECZUMSJGZH
OAGRRNCLEWKQGTJGSGRALLA
SMSPUHENWAAWYELLOMNAESM
ZRTRGRPDNNANNAEPTAEIASK
HOEIAANMINUAITACCWESSEJ
INIMSWHUMARTINGARDNEREA
UWNEAARHATREHSIRDIVADGC
TWEWKTASXOENDAELVANWAHO
DDEZIZZEMNPREHTALONOINE
IERRAJHIAKCHAMMMERLOCKL
KRD SFVOMSKOORETTAWEA
WAN GOENCREHPOSOLIHPP
JUU WYNOKROTHUEWAERDH
KQJACANDAGOACATIKSAXTOZ
ASTECTHNCUSTEDHNODRATLT
IAMTHEDANISMCREECOUEJLHA

Trees

On this our earth, "this goodly frame" as Hamlet calls it, we have the great good fortune to be accompanied in our mad spinning through space by magnificent, wise, and mighty beings call trees. Any tree can offer solace or advice when one knows how to listen, but some trees do more than that for conjurers. When conjurers come to a decision point or a dilemma, they know they need to sit at the foot of a great tree, and most have a specific tree they need to visit.

What happens between tree and conjurer varies. Some describe an answer rising like water from a rooted well. Others have said that the wisdom floats down from the tree's canopy, wafting randomly toward them, like a falling leaf.

PETERGREEN
THING
QUICKS?
JAREDKINCAID
SCULPTOR
EMPATHEE

Music

In the ancient conjuring scrolls salvaged from Pompeii, the great Adamadel writes "Only one power can rival that of conjuring. It is the power of music." This fragment has started many an argument between conjurers wanting to interpret or discredit it.

Regardless of the power of music, the effect of music on conjurers is powerful, and many seek it out. Music displacement allows conjurers to attend any concert in history, with Fourth Century druid solstice concerts at Stonehenge among the most frequented. Conjurers report feeling renewed inspiration for their arts after drinking in the music there, and some, though they are not universally believed, claim their conjuring effects gain power.

∩Kꟿꟽ∨Γ∽∽∩
ꓤꓱꓛꓶꓕꓠOH
ꟿOꙄꓠꓩOOꓤꓤ
ꓕꓠꙄHⱵꓶꓴꟽ
IⴸꓤꗧHIꓕꓜ
∪ꓤꓱꓶꓘꓤꟽꓠ
ᐸꓕꓱOƷOHᐱ
ꟽOꓷꓠOꓱꟿ∪

01011010&01011010>PU001
0SUNAMCMWERDNAVDPGGP211
0SIWLLKY1035LAWJICKL001
0UM<MN>WHHSNAIRAR3IL110
0PP>HZUWZNOXFRDZNHVE221
0YPMOHCOOPERUEN1SRUVDEW
0DIDAVPIFTMOW>HHIMWUDWH
0THURSTONNAPROXIMATESKY
0WRHYRREKIHCTA3MOTDAMDP
ZWRPMSCIUMN>RDSROCKSTAR
<>RWZHWH3RONGIEREVOSRSL
ERIVNFLOCKS 3USTER3ERRY
MKMRDRMPHP HDZHWMKZOH
CONJURERUMI ARWWLHW<R<S
WA<DRH<ZWUR<MTRWW3AJTAK
3GA3YWEIDLINGWWNSARAMAI
ILRIM CSRH>HSHL>R CMOMU
KOCU WDO D3Z ERRP
MWHRS ZMPL LLPJ DSLD>
HFKEUCRHZL HNREKOJGLC
HON3P<S>WALMLIZLLAFEEHL
HRIMGL>U3NFOLPYUHDONNWN
NGGIR>R> DITDR ALEXMIS>
PEHLUU> POI WIKCLWD
HWTCDHWH CDMS♥ R<WUKGRH
>>ZR<WM>IS3RANDONNOE3KM
NRZIZHHRDWKIM<WCS3ZNRHW
11WAHR<>DJWV3IDDUVCZZRO
44ILTWINHRRDREAYNSDWHIMHK
00>DSL<PWHDSTCNPDZNSE6IL
22DRHWRMPCSDH<ZWUIRHSHO

Foods

Conjurers don't often crave conviviality, but when they do, displacement allows them to choose from a buffet of feasts and friends. One group of conjurers gathers from around the world in May and October at Dionysian festivals in Greece to unwind and celebrate, while the Conjuring Collective holds its decennial meetings at the wedding feast of Maria de Medici and Henry IV of England in 1600.

Modayna, a Filipina conjurer, dines every Saturday morning at the annual Sinulog Fluvial breakfast at Cebú. There are so many places to choose from that she has more than enough to fill her Saturdays until the next festival. She describes her practice as an indulgence of sweet rice, mango, and hot chocolate dipping sauces not available in the country where she currently resides.

Metamagic

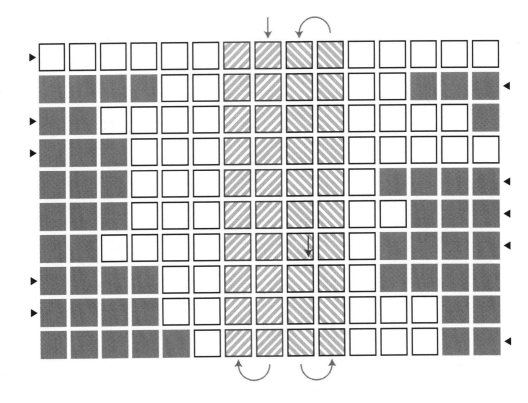

Few people even know that conjurers exist. Many that do think they are just magicians. But real conjurers know the difference!

Magicians, in a word, are charlatans. Some are talented, but it's just a show, sleight of hand, a trick, a deception, smoke and mirrors, an illusion, a chimera of sorts. Not. Real.

Conjuring, on the other hand, is the real thing. As this volume has well illustrated, conjurers do what others deem to be impossible. Teleport from one place to another. Transmute elements. Harness the powers of the earth. Cause personal epiphanies.

What is little known, however, is that magicians and conjurers have a long, shared history. Our ancient brethren had very few powers, and they didn't understand even the powers they did have very well. Their people needed to believe in and benefit from their powers, but, similar to our times, people couldn't believe in something they couldn't perceive with their five senses. Out of necessity, they augmented those powers with deceptions, which were, in essence, smoke without mirrors.

Over time, the magic arts and the conjuring arts diverged. Magicians forgot what little real magic they knew, and conjurers eschewed anything that wasn't real. The words diverged, too. With only one exception, conjurers never talk about what they do as "magic."

The one exception is metamagic. Why this word survived is lost in the mists of time! Perhaps it was the alliteration! Metamagic is the most advanced of all the conjuring arts, and there is only time to briefly touch upon it in this volume.

In metamagic, conjurers summon everything they've learned from multiple conjuring arts in order to do things that are utterly impossible with any single form of conjuring.

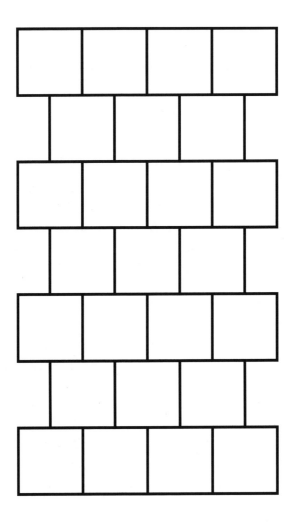

One reason that metamagic is so difficult is that there are few, if any, instructions on how to use it. These rather limited notes may be the first such instructions!

Metamagic is extremely hard but it is also extremely rewarding. It is not, however, rewarding if a conjurer has not fully mastered all of the arts. In this ultimate test of conjuring, a sort of a final exam, a conjurer will use every single conjuring art at their disposal.

Metamagic is performed using a framework of knowledge. There are many types of metamagic frameworks, and the conjurer must choose an appropriate one for the task at hand. Two particular types of frameworks are useful for illustrative purposes.

In a *Direct Knowledge* framework, a conjurer explicitly combines key information they have learned from each of the conjuring arts that they have mastered in order to learn some new information. While the conjurer will have to figure out what goes where within such a framework, directional guidance is provided. When the framework is complete, the new knowledge will reveal itself.

A *Diagonal Knowledge* framework is easier to use, but significantly harder to prepare for. Its use starts with knowledge learned from a Direct Knowledge framework and its result is a spell or counterspell. The conjurer must first interpret and learn from this new knowledge, then search out, diagonally, the additional information needed to fill the framework, wherever it may be. In the process, they will once again use all of the conjuring arts. Once the proper information is determined, it is a simple matter to place it in the framework in its natural order, exactly one item per row, and the intended result will reveal itself. At this point, a skilled conjurer will know what to do next.

Conjurers who master metamagic can write their own ticket to a brilliant career, while those who cannot may remain trapped.

Conjurer's Codes

Over the years, conjurers have created tens of thousands of codes, and more are invented all the time. Conjurers use code systems to help them perform and preserve the arts, keeping necessary secrets out of prying eyes.

Most codes, as well as their creators, are little known outside of conjuring circles, and many have been lost over the years. The Amazing Axolotl's Leaping Dragon code has only survived in fables and handed-down legend. Only a handful of conjurers still alive have ever read messages in The Great Rose-Linaria's Floral code. It has been reported that Floral messages were incredibly beautiful in the springtime.

Although many conjurer's codes are extremely complex (witness those created by the conjurers known as Emmy Noether and Hedy Lamarr!), plenty are simple enough that even a beginning conjurer can master them. This section contains some of the most useful codes, including ones created by the conjurers known as Samuel Morse, Louis Braille, Claude Chappe, and Arthur Conan Doyle.

Astrology

Aries	Taurus	Gemini	Cancer
Leo	Virgo	Libra	Scorpio
Sagittarius	Capricorn	Aquarius	Pisces
Sun	Mercury	Venus	Earth
Moon	Mars	Ceres	Jupiter
Saturn	Uranus	Neptune	Pluto

Braille

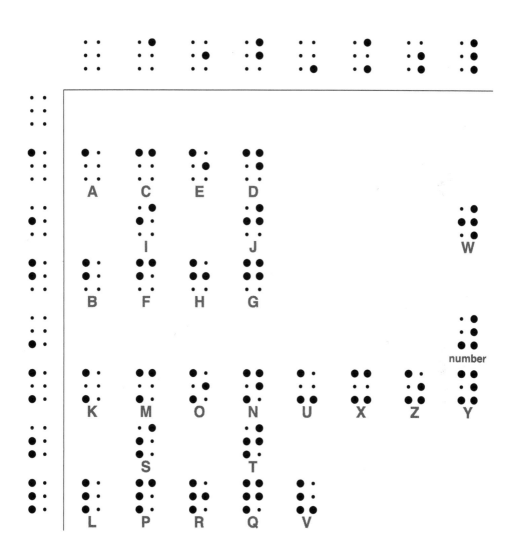

Dancing Men

A1   B2   C3   D4   E5

F6   G7   H8   I9   J0

K   L   M   N   O

P   Q   R   S   T

U   V   W   X   Y   Z

Morse

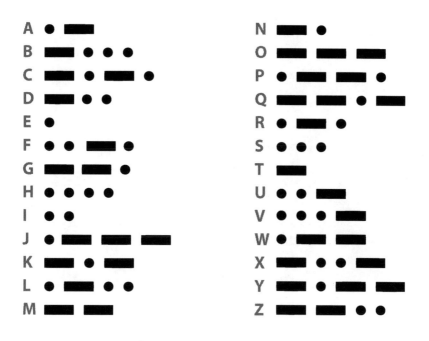

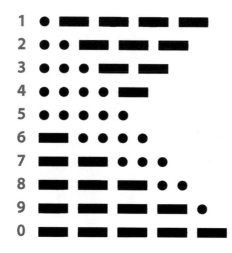

Nautical Flags

Semaphore

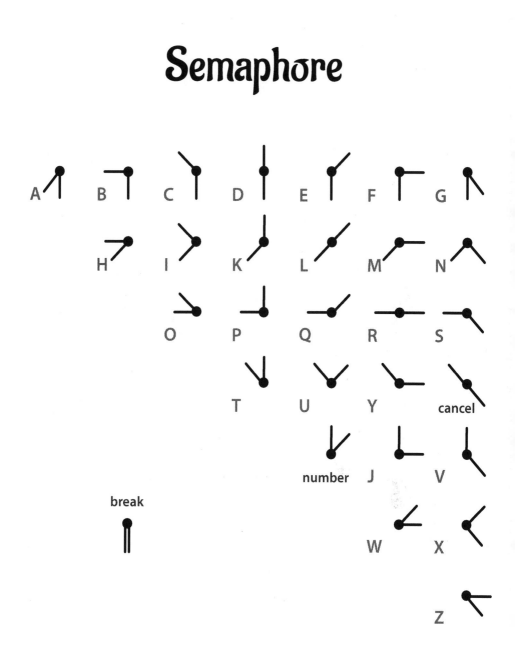

Pigpen

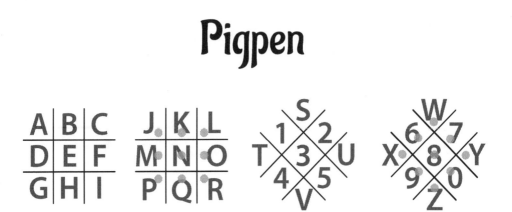

Templar

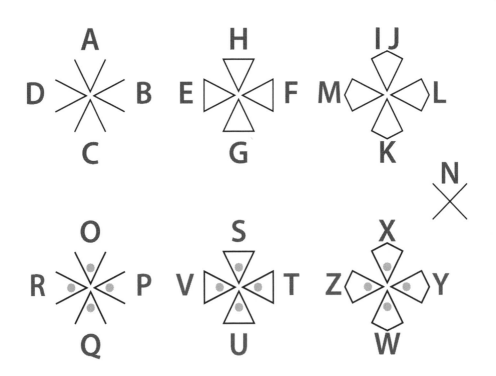

Word Alphabets

NATO	**Western Union**
Alfa	Adams
Bravo	Boston
Charlie	Chicago
Delta	Denver
Echo	Easy
Foxtrot	Frank
Golf	George
Hotel	Henry
India	Ida
Juliet	John
Kilo	King
Lima	Lincoln
Mike	Mary
November	New York
Oscar	Ocean
Papa	Peter
Quebec	Queen
Romeo	Roger
Sierra	Sugar
Tango	Thomas
Uniform	Union
Victor	Victor
Whiskey	William
X-ray	X-ray
Yankee	Young
Zulu	Zero

Acknowledgements

The Conjurer's Almanaq would not exist without the help of many people! This group includes advisors, reviewers, test solvers, plus people who inspired us, as well as the guest constructors for the companion booklet, *The Morgue*. Although the precise role of many of them necessarily must remain secret, you can find their names or noms in this volume.

We appreciate the support of all of our Kickstarter backers as well as our post-campaign "last chance" backers. We have included the names or noms of those Kickstarter backers at the Signed Softcover level and above.

Some icons used in *The Conjurer's Almanaq* are from The Noun Project. Some items pictured were made on Glowforge.

It goes without saying that we are deeply indebted to The Great Qdini himself for creating this Almanaq in the first place, despite the spell he later placed upon it. And, of course, we could not possibly have published this facsimile edition of the fabled original, had it not been for the amazing conjurer, whose name we have promised to withhold, whose initial escape from this very volume helped us free ourselves when we were trapped. She has saved us all!

Colophon

The Conjurer's Almanaq is set in Baskerville, with titles set in Aladin. The Displacement matrixes are set in the **WIM** font. Additional fonts include Helvetica Neue, Myriad Pro, Times New Roman, and Courier New. Software used included Adobe Illustrator and Photoshop, Microsoft Word and Excel, and custom programs created by Roy.

Special Offers

Puzzazz has two special offers for solvers of *The Conjurer's Almanaq.*

Get a free puzzle book in the Puzzazz app (up to a $3 value, one per person) by using the Potions answer as a redemption code. In the Puzzazz app, every book starts with at least one free puzzle. Solve some of them to decide which book you want. Once you've chosen a book, visit http://www.puzzazz.com/redeem and enter the code, then choose the book you'd like to get for free. To download the Puzzazz app for your iPad, iPhone, or iPod Touch, visit http://www.puzzazz.com/ituneslink

Get a 20% discount on Puzzazz's Year of Puzzles, a puzzlehunt of 22 unique puzzles edited by Roy Leban, with puzzles by Roy and:

- Will Shortz
- Ken Jennings
- Patrick Berry
- Thomas Snyder
- Mike Shenk
- Richard Garfield
- Mike Selinker
- Joshua Kosman
- Henri Picciotto
- Dan Katz
- Eric Harshbarger
- Bruce Leban
- Parker Lewis
- *story by* Emily Dietrich
- *art by* Jill Schmidt

Puzzles can be solved in the Puzzazz app or via printable PDFs.

For more information on the Year of Puzzles, visit http://www.puzzazz.com/yearofpuzzles/almanaq

Also from Almanaq

The Librarian's Almanaq
by Roy Leban

The Librarian's Almanaq is the culmination of Literally centuries Of tremendous work by a dedicated team Of researchers who just couldn't Keep it under wraps. Here, you'll get the advice you need to be successful in the World and learn the *sine qua non* of puzzledom. Never before has a wealth of Information like This been gathered in one place, let alone a single volume. Your Hunger for sacred knowledge can finally be sated! Examine the Almanaq carefully and make sure to read the Instructions, and you can turn onto a New path toward enlightenment.

The Librarian's Almanaq is an all-in-one puzzlehunt, an interconnected suite of a dozen unique and fun puzzles, culminating in a satisfying conclusion, and all put together in a form you've never seen before. You might find a live duck handy.

The Morgue
edited by Roy Leban and Emily Dietrich

The Morgue is a standalone 32-page facsimile booklet of seemingly unrelated newspaper clippings, saved by The Great Qdini, and discovered after he vanished. Why did he save these particular clippings? Nobody knows! Maybe you'll be the one to figure it out!

This is a companion book to *The Conjurer's Almanaq*, containing 20 puzzles by guest constructors combined with an overall metapuzzle.

Visit www.almanaq.com for more information

Made in the USA
Las Vegas, NV
07 December 2021

36486017R00139